THE RISE OF ASIAN PAINTS

Cartoonist R.K. Laxman's sketch of Champaklal Choksey

THE RISE OF ASIAN PAINTS

CHAMPAKLAL CHOKSEY, A DOYEN OF THE INDIAN PAINTS INDUSTRY

ANUPAM GUPTA

PENGUIN
BUSINESS

An imprint of Penguin Random House

PENGUIN BUSINESS

Penguin Business is an imprint of the Penguin Random House group of companies whose addresses can be found at global.penguinrandomhouse.com

Published by Penguin Random House India Pvt. Ltd
4th Floor, Capital Tower 1, MG Road,
Gurugram 122 002, Haryana, India

Penguin
Random House
India

First published in Penguin Business by Penguin Random House India 2024

Images courtesy: author

10 9 8 7 6 5 4 3 2 1

ISBN 9780670097982

Typeset in Sabon Lt Std by MAP Systems, Bengaluru, India
Printed at Thomson Press India Ltd, New Delhi

www.penguin.co.in

Disclaimer: This book is a biography of Champaklal Choksey, one of the four founding partners of Asian Paints. It has been written after extensive interviews with the Choksey family, with some of his friends and well-wishers, as well as with a few employees who worked in his era, and with other industry experts. This book relies on data and materials from annual reports, newspaper archives and various other sources. This book also relies on an older, undated biography that was written in Gujarati for Champakbhai's family, titled *Champakbhai Choksey: Another Name for Asian (Paints)*. Sources have been attributed for reference and all efforts have been made to ensure authenticity.

Contents

Foreword

When I migrated to India in 2008, I didn't know much about Asian Paints or Champaklal Choksey (CHC). Having spent my childhood in India, I had heard of the Asian Paints brand but had no idea of its truly unique origin story. During my first decade of living in India, I began delving deeper into the company's history and gradually became a CHC buff. In my travels around India, as I would track down ex-Asian Paints employees and try to understand the evolution of the company, CHC's name would inevitably come up.

In 2016, I authored a book, *The Unusual Billionaires,* which spoke about some unique companies in India that have had a 10 per cent revenue growth and 15 per cent return on capital every year for ten consecutive years. Chapter Two of the book was the culmination of my first few years of research on Asian Paints.

In the same book, I wrote that Asian Paints stands out as an exemplary case study of a home-grown brand taking on competition (domestic and foreign) and winning in India. It is also a rare example of a large Indian company, owned by multiple promoter families and yet run by a high-calibre, professional management team. The firm's remarkable consistency in revenue growth, earnings growth and disciplined capital deployment stands testimony to the calibre of both the promoters and the management team. All of that has stood the test of time. One of the reasons my parents and I are Asian Paints shareholders, alongside 9000 of Marcellus's clients, is because we reckon Asian Paints will continue to excel in the years to come.

Asian Paints is more than eighty years old. Since going public in 1982, the company's share price has compounded over 20,000 times. And yet, this market-leading paints company is growing at a pace that would make smaller companies blanche; it is making capital allocation decisions that most Indian companies would envy; and it is doing so with the same set of founding families, except for CHC. It is held in high esteem by graduates from India's best B-schools and is a highly sought-after employer. This is ample testimony to the founders' vision of building a company that would outlast all of them.

This is rare in family-owned businesses because most promoters struggle to see beyond their self-interest. Even if they do, their families—indeed, their successors—might not have the same vision as the founders. When they do have the vision, success goes to their head, prompting them to make capital allocation decisions driven by ego instead of hard, financial logic. Very few Indian companies, therefore, transition into institutions in their own right—surviving and thriving as market leaders for very long periods of time. It is in this context that I found Asian Paints to be an exceptional Indian firm.

When I think of CHC and Asian Paints, I am often reminded of Deepak Parekh, who similarly built an institution—the Housing Development Finance Corporation (HDFC Limited), which merged with HDFC Bank in 2023. Following the merger, Deepakbhai closed his farewell speech with a memorable line: 'Our history cannot be erased and our legacy will be taken forward.' I think that CHC would agree with the spirit and words of such a simple yet powerful line. (Note: My parents and I alongside Marcellus's clients are also shareholders in HDFC Bank.)

Champakbhai was born in 1916. In an era that gave us legends such as J.R.D. Tata (1904), Kamalnayan Bajaj (1915) and Basant Kumar Birla (1921), Champakbhai stands right next to all of them as a titan of Indian industries. He must be remembered in the same vein as his contemporaries as they all took their businesses and made them institutions that outlived them. Champakbhai was thus a leader amongst men and a pillar of the business community in Mumbai as well as India.

In 2018, Anupam and I teamed up to write *The Victory Project*, a book focused on helping driven people achieve peak potential using a framework of principles like simplicity, specialization and spirituality built around disciplines like creativity, decluttering and teamwork. To our surprise, *The Victory Project* went on to become a national bestseller, and Anupam became a highly sought-after writer. A couple of years ago when Anupam and I met to brainstorm what he could work on next, I suggested he consider becoming CHC's biographer.

I believed that CHC's story needed to be told so other Indian entrepreneurs could learn from his journey. Fortunately, when Anupam and I reached out to CHC's son, Atul Choksey, Atulbhai was not just happy to green-light the endeavour but also to support the venture by introducing Anupam to the Choksey family and their well-wishers.

There are many lessons for entrepreneurs and family businesses in CHC's story. Investments in technology seem like an obvious thing today but was a leap of faith back in the early 1970s for CHC. Hiring professional talent is another decision that worked well for CHC. For family businesses, it could be tough to trust outsiders. But over the last fifty years, CHC and the founders of Asian Paints have demonstrated that a strong bench of professional talent is instrumental in building an invigorative work culture that then becomes a competitive advantage in its own right.

But the most valuable lesson, in my opinion, is the discipline around capital allocation. Many youngsters dream of start-ups with the plethora of funding options available today. None of these options were available to CHC, yet he and his friends worked hard to foster a disciplined system of free cashflows that sustained daily operations at first and then funded Asian Paints' expansion. As this book shows, this was neither simple nor easy and required many tough decisions, but the hard work of the founders in the early years went on to pay handsome dividends, literally and figuratively. This should serve as an example to contemporary entrepreneurs—a sensible approach towards capital allocation is the only way a business can sustain itself and succeed in the long run.

Two years after my initial chat with Anupam on this subject, I found myself reading the first draft of his biography of CHC. As luck would have it, I started reading in the opening hour of a seventeen-hour flight from Mumbai to Seattle. By the time I landed, not only did I finish reading the superbly written book but I was richer and wiser thanks to the learnings embedded in this outstanding narrative on a legendary entrepreneur. I hope you enjoy this biography as much as I did.

Mumbai, 3 January 2024

Saurabh Mukherjea,
founder and chief investment officer, Marcellus Investment Managers

Prologue

Mumbai, 31 July 1997

It was like any other Thursday in Mumbai. A low-pressure area that formed over the Bay of Bengal on the previous day had moved west to Mumbai showering the metropolis with bountiful rains and helping to fill the lakes nearby that supplied water to the city. The BSE Sensex closed at 4305.76 points, up by a healthy 22 per cent over the previous year. Most of these gains would be wiped out in the next year thanks to the Asian financial crisis of 1997.

That Thursday in July 1997 began like any other at Geetanjali, the residence of the Chokseys, one of the four partners who owned and controlled Asian Paints, India's largest paints company. Located less than a kilometre away from the famous Mahalaxmi Temple in South Mumbai, Geetanjali is a nine-storey building nestled on the gentle slopes in Cumballa Hill.

The Choksey family was then in its third generation, which had seen two marriages in the recent past, that of Ankur in 1995 and Prashant in 1996. Ankur and Prashant are the sons of Girish Choksey, the eldest son of the family patriarch, Champaklal Hiralal Choksey. In Gujarati, the words 'bhai' (brother) and 'ben' (sister) are suffixed to names out of love and respect, usually to all grown-ups but especially for senior members of the family; so Champaklal was Champakbhai.

Born in 1916, Champakbhai Choksey was fondly known simply as CHC or Champak Seth[1] within Asian Paints and

[1] 'Seth' in Hindi means a rich businessman.

Champakbhai in the paints industry. In less than a month, Champakbhai would turn eighty-one. Despite his old age and faltering health (he'd had a bypass surgery in 1988), he celebrated Ankur's and Prashant's weddings with the joyful happiness of a grandfather seeing his grandsons move to the next phase of their lives.

The financial year that ended on 31 March 1997 was unremarkable for the paint industry, with just 7 per cent growth, due to many reasons such as a slowdown in consumer goods demand, tight credit conditions, and protests against new taxes and legislations in different parts of the country. All these factors affected dealer offtake, as per the 1997 Asian Paints annual report.

And yet, FY1996–97 was not even a blip in Asian Paints' long and storied history. In what would turn out to be his last letter to shareholders, Champakbhai sounded upbeat and enthusiastic looking ahead. He wrote, 'Happily, the times we live in have opportunities aplenty. As the economy gathers momentum, there is bound to be a manifold increase in the potentially beneficial courses of action open to us.'

Formed in 1942, Asian Paints became the largest paints industry player in India by 1967—a position it holds comfortably even today. In 1982, Asian Paints offered shares to the public, and if you were lucky enough to snag ten shares at the offer price of Rs 23 per share and had been sensible enough to not sell a single one, then by 1997 you would have held seventy-seven shares (after four bonus issues from 1982 to 1997) which were trading at Rs 280 each by 31 March that year. So, your investment of Rs 230 would be worth Rs 21,504, up ninety-three times from your initial investment of Rs 230—an astounding 36 per cent compound annual growth rate (CAGR) over fifteen years till 31 March 1997.

Asian Paints' share price was simply tracking the financial performance of the company and the high standards set by the four promoters, namely the Danis, Chokseys, Choksis and

Vakils (in alphabetical order). Two friends—Suryakantbhai Dani and Champakbhai Choksey—started a paints trading agency in 1942, and they were joined by Arvindbhai Vakil and Chimanbhai Choksi. The four friends charted an aggressive expansion for Asian Paints from a garage in South Mumbai to a modern facility in Bhandup in 1958.

Champakbhai Choksey and his partners were smarter and bolder than the competition they faced in the form of large multinational companies and small unorganized players. They raced ahead of both, in the process creating a giant that rules at #1 even today. Starting with what looked like small ideas (targeting product gaps like painting the horns of bulls in regional festivals) to taking early and audacious bets on computerization and hiring highly trained professionals, Asian Paints outsmarted their competition. With effective advertising and iconic ad campaigns, Asian Paints firmly entrenched itself as a brand that customers would ask for at shops.

Asian Paints never rested on its laurels. It kept expanding and increasing the gap between itself and its competitors. By the 1980s and 1990s, Asian Paints opened three new facilities (Ankleshwar, Patancheru and Kasna), tied up with foreign players for technology, reduced costs by integrating backward and—in one of its most famous achievements—mastered the art of the supply chain. In doing all of this, Champakbhai and his fellow founders set the course for the company to become an institution and outlive them.

And in 1997, Champakbhai was the last remaining of the original four founders, with his friends and partners having passed away in earlier years. The second generation was assuming command. Atul Choksey and Ashwin Choksi were both managing directors in FY1996–97. Champakbhai and the founders mutually agreed to let only one member from each of the four families remain in senior executive roles at Asian Paints. Most of the company then was run by highly educated professionals in senior roles, such as R.B. Tirodkar (in technical), Bharat Puri (marketing) and K.B.S. Anand (Kasna and Patancheru plants).

Thus, by 1997, Champakbhai and the founders of Asian Paints successfully created one of India's largest home-grown consumer brands that led its competitors by a country mile. But Asian Paints' achievements went beyond just the consumer sector. It was counted right next to the Reliance and L&Ts of India as being a very rare breed of Indian-owned, Indian-led companies that could potentially become multinational companies. This was a unique feat considering it was just six years since the 1991 economic reforms. The stock price appreciation, thus, simply mirrored the result of the hard work and dedication that Champakbhai and the founders had put into their company.

Their efforts were rewarded by the stock market. By the end of July 1997, Asian Paints' stock price climbed up to around Rs 350 per share, valuing the company at a market capitalization of more than Rs 1400 crore. All four partners held roughly the same stake, with the Chokseys holding a marginally lower stake of around 9 per cent, pegging the value of their holding at around Rs 130 crore.

On Thursday, 31 July 1997, Champakbhai Choksey sold his stake in Asian Paints to two large foreign institutional investors, Morgan Stanley and Capital International. However, as per news reports, both investors claimed that they did not know the stake they were buying belonged to the Choksey family. Within a few weeks, in a rare event in Mumbai's stock markets, the transaction was cancelled. To make things even more dramatic, Champakbhai passed away in Pune on the same Thursday that he sold his stake to the investors.

Atul Choksey then sold his stake to ICI (UK) via one of India's eminent investment bankers, Uday Kotak. ICI was a giant globally, but in India, they were a relatively smaller competitor to Asian Paints. Owning a large stake in Asian Paints would boost ICI's Indian presence. This created a furore and outrage in India over the possibility of a British multinational competitor taking over a home-grown, highly successful Indian brand. In the months to follow, regulators as well as Asian Paints successfully blocked the sale, and ICI (UK) could never own Asian Paints.

'We really cannot fathom why Champakbhai sold his stake in 1997. Why would he want to leave such a great company that he himself helped build and gave most of his life for?' This was the most commonly asked question among the many people, including CEOs and ex-employees, I spoke to for the purposes of this book.

To understand why this visionary entrepreneur sold his stake, we need to go back to the origins of Asian Paints and understand the firm's evolution.

Champakbhai Choksey Timeline

Year	Event
28 August 1916	Champaklal Hiralal Choksey is born.
1934/35	Solanki introduces Champakbhai to Suryakantbhai.
1936 to 1939	Champakbhai leaves his family home in Mumbai. Suryakantbhai offers a paint agency (of Pranjeevanbhai Vasani) partnership to Solanki who declines and offers it to Champakbhai who takes the offer. Thus Neptune Trading Agency begins.
1939	World War II begins.
1940	Champakbhai marries Kumudben.
1939/40	Neptune Trading Agency hits Rs 19,000 in sales, becoming Pranjeevanbhai's biggest dealer.
1940 to 1942	Suryakantbhai and Champakbhai decide to start their own venture and look for partners. Chimanbhai Choksi and Arvindbhai Vakil join them.
9 November 1942	Asian Oil and Paint Company is born in a garage on Foras Road. As sales increased, this facility was shifted later to Girgaum.
1945	World War II ends; Asian Oil and Paint Company (India) Limited converted to a company from a partnership.
1947	Champakbhai marries Ashvinaben, Kumudben's younger sister, following Kumudben's demise.
1947	Production shifted from Girgaum to a new factory in Matunga.
1958	Bhandup factory production starts.
1965	Company's name changed to Asian Paints (India) Private Limited.

1971	Champakbhai suffers a heart attack.
1973	Company's name changed to Asian Paints (India) Limited; Atul Choksey joins Asian Paints.
1980	Taloja plant and Ankleshwar plants begin production, overseas ventures commence in Fiji and Tonga Islands.
1982	Asian Paints (India) Limited IPO offers shares for Rs 23 (face value Rs 10).
1983	Nepal and Solomon Islands ventures commence.
1984	Atul Choksey becomes managing director, Pentasia Joint Venture (JV) with TIDCO, JV with Devoe Marine.
1985	Patancheru plant begins production.
1986	JV with Nippon, Apcotex subsidiary in Taloja, phthalic anhydride in Ankleshwar.
1988	Champakbhai undergoes a bypass surgery under Dr Denton Cooley in the US.
1990	Kasna plant begins production.
1991	Apcotex separated/de-merged from Asian Paints.
1993	Pentasia goes to Board for Industrial and Financial Reconstruction (BIFR) and eventually merges with Asian Paints in 1996.
1994	Vanuatu and Australia ventures commence.
1996	Mauritius venture commences, fire at Bhandup plant.
31 July 1997	Champakbhai sells the Choksey family stake in Asian Paints and passes away.

(Source: Annual reports, family records.)

The Champaklal Choksey Family Tree

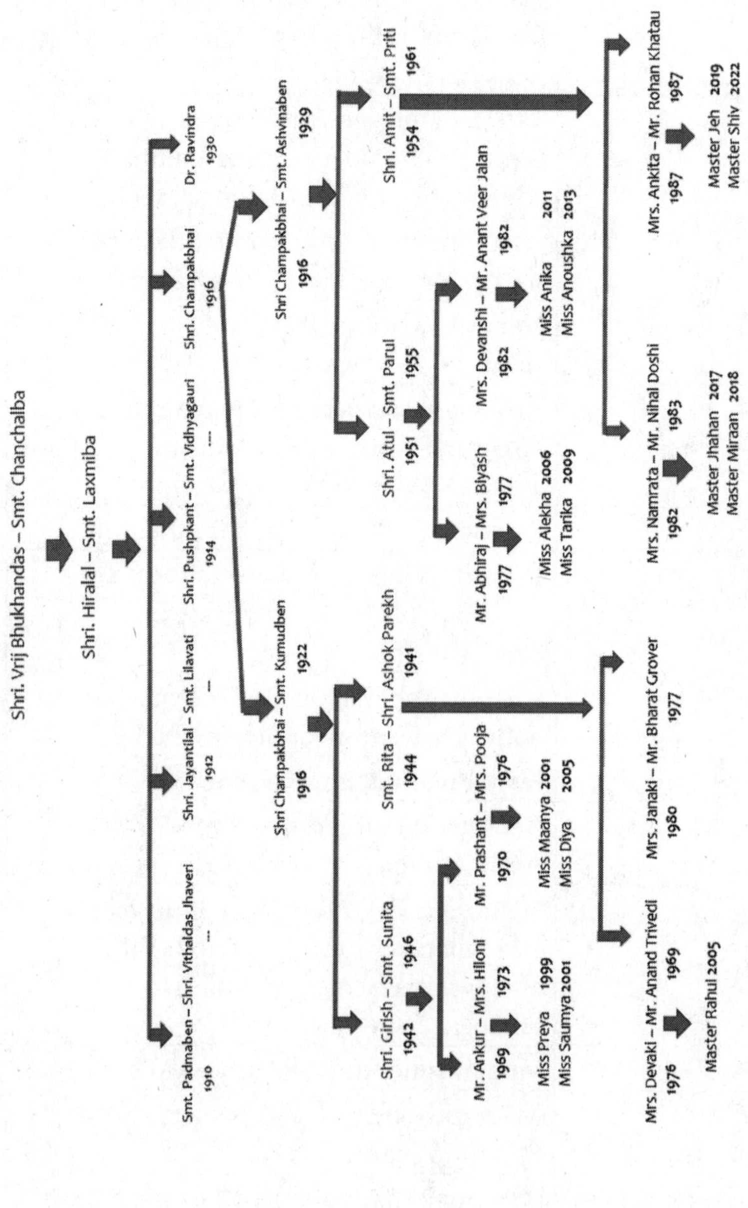

Part 1

The Early Years

Chapter 1

A Volatile Youth

'Youth has no age.'

—Pablo Picasso

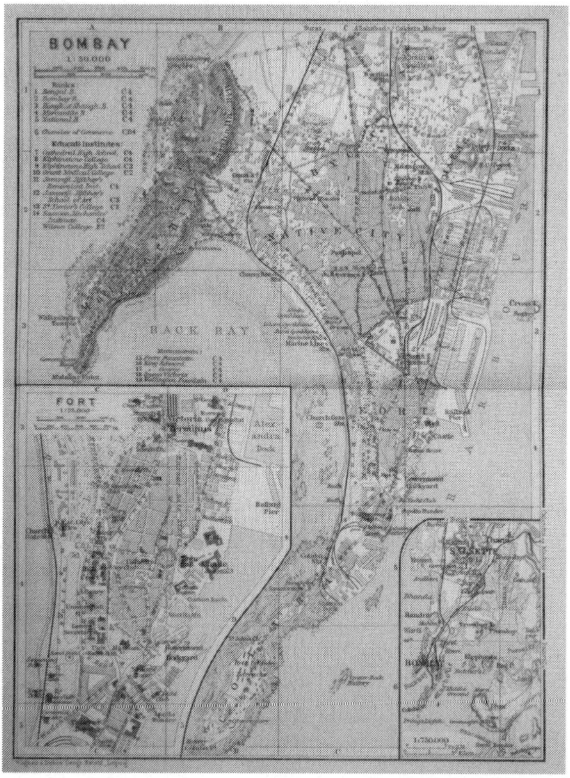

Map of Bombay, 1949

(Credit: Wikimedia Creative Commons)

Champaklal Hiralal Choksey was born on 28 August 1916 to Shri Hiralal Vrijbhukandas Parmananddas Choksey and Shrimati Madangauri Choksey. In their earlier generations, the Chokseys went by surnames such as Nanavati and Shroff (usually linked to their profession, vocation, community, group, etc.) before finally settling on Choksey. He was the fourth of five children, namely three sons and two daughters (see the Choksey family tree). The Chokseys belonged to the Bhavanivad area in Surat, one of the largest cities in the state of Gujarat. Their home was located at Ghee Kanta Road in Haripura (a neighbourhood in Bhavanivad), about three kilometres away from the Tapi River that flows through Madhya Pradesh, Maharashtra and Gujarat. Surat is the world's largest diamond manufacturing centre with areas like Palanpur that are famous for diamond polishing. It is not known exactly when Hiralal left Surat for Bombay (as it was known then) where Champaklal was born in 1916.

Champakbhai was born in the heady days of business in Bombay. The benefits of the Industrial Revolution had pushed India from trade and commerce to industry in the late 1800s. Cotton production was among the earliest beneficiaries of mechanization in the 1800s, and by the 1900s, this trend spread across other commodities. While Indian businessmen had replaced Britishers in cotton production, the British still controlled other major commodities.

But just as the American Civil War gave a major boost to the production of cotton in India, World War I and the disruption of imports provided a huge opportunity for Indian businesses to set up factories beyond cotton. This extract from master corporate historian, the late Dwijendra Tripathi, in his tome *The Oxford History of Indian Business* puts the scale and size of India's entrepreneurs and expatriates into perspective during this era, 'How much had the Indian business scene changed during the period (the last quarter of the previous century) is clear from the fact that by the end of the nineteenth century, there were as many as 627 firms with a total paid-up capital of over Rs 2500 lakh that were engaged in some kind of manufacturing activities. Just about two decades ago, the number was limited to 264 companies with a total paid-up capital of [a] little less than Rs 1100 lakh.'

Bombay—Fertile Ground for Industry

Industrialization in Bombay had already begun in the 1850s and 1860s when Bombay became the largest cotton market in India.[1] By this time, the seven islands were merged to form one contiguous mass, and the launch of the locomotive-powered train between Thane and Bombay in 1853 (just twenty years after the first train rolled out in Britain) further boosted the prospects for business. Alongside the laying of rail tracks was the development of the docks in Bombay, from Sassoon Dock to Prince's and Victoria Docks. To add to the trains and docks, was the stock market, which, famously, came into being when a bunch of traders came together to trade in stocks in the 1850s under a banian tree in Horniman Circle, opposite the Asiatic Society.

All of this rapid development of business was happening in the area now known as South Mumbai, which today loosely covers everything from Colaba to Mahim in the west and Sion in the east.

Nestled within South Mumbai and a few kilometres north of Colaba, running parallel to the local train tracks are a bunch of localities known as Kalbadevi, Bhuleshwar and Girgaum which were native towns in their own right with their respective histories. Smaller localities called *gaothans* and *padas* were named after the communities (e.g. Agripada), Gods (e.g. Kalbadevi which was a major area for wholesale trading

---

[1] Mayabhushan Nagvenkar, *The Boom and Bust of Bombay Mills*, 22 July 2022, Outlook, https://www.outlookindia.com/national/the-boom-and-bust-of-bombay-mills-news-211684.

of commodities) and geography (e.g. Girgaum or village at the foot of the hills).

As the cotton business boomed, people like Hiralal Choksey migrated to Bombay from various parts of India. Hiralal traded in cotton in Surat and on the cotton exchange in Bombay. He lived close to the cotton market (or Kapda Bazaar) in South Mumbai, in an area between Charni Road (the third local train station after Churchgate and Marine Lines on the local train network) and Girgaum, known as Gaiwadi (*Gai* is the Hindi word for cow and Gaiwadi possibly comes from the cows grazing in that area).

Next to Gaiwadi is another locality called Kandawadi ('kanda' is the Marathi and Gujarati word for onion), which again suggests a horti/agricultural origin. Today, the Gaiwadi and Kandawadi areas are known for printing wedding cards, and if you drive by the very narrow lanes (made even narrower today with the Mumbai Metro Rail construction), you will go past a building colony whose entrance has 'Gaiwadi' written on it and has gates in the shape of two cows with bells around their necks—one cow on the right and one on the left—as if to welcome visitors. These are the areas where Champakbhai grew up and spent his days as a child.

I met the veteran senior heritage activist and researcher, Jagdish Gandhi, at his ornate home in Santa Cruz to understand how the Girgaum area evolved over time. Pointing me to his beautifully detailed book, *A Tale of Native Towns of Mumbai* (self-published in 2010), Jagdish told me how communities across economic strata came to Mumbai in search of vocations and professions. In his book, Gandhi writes, 'During the British era, the textile industry acted as an engine of India's industrial growth. In its wake, it triggered an influx of labour from the rural areas. It also opened up clerical and high-level administrative opportunities for the rural educated class. These immigrants, belonging to all classes and strata of society, needed to be housed. This need of the time found its response in the chawl system of housing. Long lines of chawls came up in the

Lalbaug, Parel, Elphinstone and Mazgaon areas to house the labour class, mostly the *girni* (textile mills) workers. The chawls in Girgaum catered to a better-educated class of people who were either officegoers, professionals or small shop owners.'

Volatile Temperament

Hiralal Choksey and his family stayed in one such chawl system, or *maalo* (nest in Gujarati) known as 'Tambakuvalo Malo' (possibly from *tambaku*, the Hindi word for Tobacco) in Kandawadi, Girgaum. Records with the Choksey family are unclear as to the nature of Hiralal's business during this time. Champakbhai's temperament was evident even as a child. He was very friendly but also very short-tempered and refused to be bullied by kids or treated unfairly by teachers. Never one to back down from a fight, there are many incidents of Champakbhai's temper both as a child and later on as a business leader.

One such incident from his school days is as follows: he and his friends would return covered with dust and caked in mud after playing in school. When the games in school were not enough, the children sought open grounds to play in. As any resident of Mumbai will tell you even today, open and publicly accessible spaces for children are few and far between in a space-starved city. Chawls have hardly any open space within them where children can play, and the common area, usually at the entrance, doubles as a community space which is too crowded for a bunch of high-energy, restless boys.

So, one day, Champakbhai and his friends decide to land opposite their home in the garden of a house which belonged to a very famous Gujarati judge and scholar. As luck would have it, the gang of boys broke some plants and pots while playing, and this led to the wife of the judge complaining to Champakbhai's mother but eventually both families settled things amicably.

Another story is from his school. Champakbhai went to G.T. school along with his siblings, carrying a slate and chalk.

He was a good student and his favourite subjects were history and geography. When kids missed school, they had to get their homework from their friends, complete it at home and present it to the teacher the next day. So, one day when Champakbhai missed school, he asked his friend for the homework and finished it at home. What he didn't know was that his friend had played a prank on him and given him the incorrect homework. When Champakbhai presented his homework the next day to his very strict math teacher, he was punished and, despite his vociferous protests, told to stand on a bench.

Refusing to accept this punishment, Champakbhai stormed out of class and sat in the school canteen for that class and every following math class. One day, the school principal spotted Champakbhai and questioned him over his protest. Champakbhai insisted that the math teacher should personally take him back to class, and after prolonged negotiations and a confession from the child who played the prank, the math teacher accompanied Champakbhai back to class. That academic year, he scored 94/100 in math, much to the satisfaction of the teacher and the relief of Champakbhai's parents.

While the naughty streak settled down in later years, the energy and physical strength remained for a long while. Champakbhai loved wrestling and I heard many stories of his strength and prowess, from catching a thief in a neighbour's home in Surat to dealing with goons in the neighbourhood. His fearlessness would also help him in handling tough labour negotiations at the Bhandup factory. His strong presence, coupled with an easy-going, friendly but firm personality made Champakbhai popular with his friends and would eventually be one of the reasons that endeared him to his employees.

The naughty streak and zest for life would define Champakbhai, who loved to live life to the fullest. He enjoyed physical activity, and his favourite sports were cricket and tennis. When Wimbledon began being broadcast on television in India, he keenly followed the game. He loved food with a passion and his favourite food was bhajiya (fritters that accompany meals).

Champakbhai enjoyed traditional Gujarati snacks, or farsan, that came in many varieties. Once a month, a domestic help-cum-office peon named Amin was dispatched to Surat, the native city of the Chokseys and renowned for 'Surati' food. Amin would bring back many types of authentic farsan from sev-gathiya to 'bhusa' (a sweet/spicy mix of puffed and pressed rice, peanuts, cornflakes and more) that would become part of Champakbhai's meals.

Hari Prasad Solanki—An Important Link

Among all his school friends, however, Hari Prasad Solanki was very close to his heart. So close, that Champakbhai made him one of many beneficiaries in his will and remained a father figure to his family. This story has been recounted by many family members and goes like this. When he was a teenager, possibly fifteen–sixteen years old in the early 1930s, Champakbhai and his friends woke up in the morning and would go jogging together near Chowpatty, a large and popular beach in South Mumbai. They would jog from the beach to Nariman Point (one of Mumbai's business districts located at the southern tip) and back to the beach. To cool off, they would then go for a swim in the sea. Champakbhai enjoyed swimming and jogging, and swimming in the morning was a routine for him, Solanki and their group of friends. Physically, Champakbhai was tall and well built with particularly wide and strong shoulders. Add to that a piercing gaze and a booming voice, and he had a very recognizable personality that was hard to forget.

On one such morning outing at Chowpatty, Champakbhai and his friends jumped in the water and kept swimming. After a while, everyone came back except Champakbhai, much to everyone's horror. Without thinking of calling for assistance from grown-ups nearby and without hesitation, Hari Prasad Solanki ran into the waters, swam furiously, rescued Champakbhai and brought him back to shore. Their friendship lasted for life, and Champakbhai remained indebted to Solanki for saving his life. The friendship with Solanki assumes significance in Champakbhai's life because it was Solanki who would eventually introduce Champakbhai to Suryakant Chandulal Dani in what would turn out to be a key moment in Champakbhai's early life.

Solanki often visited Champakbhai at home where both friends would enjoy evenings full of tea, dhokla, farsan and many stories recounted to the Choksey family. Champakbhai helped Solanki in his career, and Solanki worked at Asian Paints for many years, initially in sales and then in exports, sitting at the Asian Paints office at Das Chambers, near the Bombay Stock Exchange building.

An Early Loss in the Family

After finishing school, Champakbhai went to Mumbai's renowned St Xavier's College to study what was then called 'Inter Science' or intermediate, roughly corresponding to high school which is before graduation. Champakbhai followed this up with a diploma course at Davar's College in South Mumbai. Champakbhai had lost his mother early in life but this never affected his studies thanks to his father. His father Hiralal requested his eldest daughter, Padmaben, to help him take care of the children. This decision would have a profound effect on Champakbhai.

Padmaben gave all her love and attention to ensure that all the Choksey children were looked after and eventually settled down. However, Hiralal could never get over the death of his wife and shut down his business. He tried working in his uncle's business, but this also did not work well for him. Champakbhai worked odd jobs to supplement his family's income through these tough times. Much to his father's consternation, he also began betting and was particularly good at cards.

In the 1900s, gambling and speculating on everything from cards to horses to commodities were legitimate occupations as long as you didn't go bankrupt. Further, playing cards is a ritual during

Janmashtami among Gujaratis.[2] Champakbhai became very good at playing cards but never let gambling become an addiction. But as Champakbhai grew old, his favourite card game would turn out to be Patience, more popularly known as Solitaire.

Patience literally requires you to patiently arrange cards in sequence in their decks after drawing them from a pack of cards. Your attention is thus divided between the deck from which cards are drawn and the stacks of cards that you have to build in sequence. Microsoft popularized Solitaire in earlier versions of their Windows operating software along with games like Minesweeper. Patience can be played alone, and as he aged, that is how Champakbhai preferred to play it, silently thinking about his next move and his plans for Asian Paints.

Champakbhai's first twenty years (1916–36) were formative in shaping his fundamental values and outlook towards life. Seeing his family's fortune decline led him to work very hard, become resilient in taking setbacks in his stride, and become determined to build a secure and unassailable base for his family in the future. His antics at school and his mercurial temper show him to be a very motivated person who could stand up against authority if he believed he was right, and was resolute against any forms of unfairness.

Having a brigade of close friends meant that Champakbhai was an easy-going and fun-loving man who loved the company of people. And finally, his education and college admission meant that Champakbhai had a reasonably good education, including a good command of spoken and written English. Over time, he honed his command of English by reading everything from newspapers to magazines and books such as *The Godfather*. Coupled with his imposing persona, his ease with English as a language would become a competitive advantage while setting

[2] Press Trust of India and *Business Standard*, 'Shuffle the Playing Cards, It's Janmashtami Again!', www.business-standard.com, 4 September 2015, https://www.business-standard.com/article/pti-stories/shuffle-the-playing-cards-it-s-janmashtami-again-115090400209_1.html.

up Asian Paints as an Indian company among foreign players. And the journey that eventually led to Asian Paints would come in the most unexpected ways to Champakbhai.

Switching Jobs

At the age of nineteen, Champakbhai's friend found him his first job out of college—at a watch company. This didn't last long since Champakbhai didn't like the idea of the owner of the shop frisking employees when they left work. He worked for three months before deciding to leave, tired of the owner's constant suspicions about the employees. Hiralal spoke to his friend, Gordhandas Surti, who was licensed to work in Bombay's huge cotton market to find work for Champakbhai as a jobber (also locally known as a *mukadam*), which was then a prestigious job.

As Professor Tirthankar Roy of the London School of Economics wrote in his research note[3] in 2008,

> Whatever their origins, in the 1920s the jobbers conducted much more than recruitment. They were effectively workers entrusted with the duties of a personnel manager, they were in charge of full utilization of the machines, and in the absence of a well-developed apprenticeship, in charge of supplying and shaping skill levels as well. The managers and owners could wash their hands of training and education precisely because the jobber was by default, but rarely in practice, in charge of these functions.

Champakbhai worked hard at this job, repaid his father's debt and improved the overall financial condition of the Choksey family. However, things within the family would soon take a turn for the worse.

---

[3] 'Labour Institutions, Japanese Competition, and the Crisis of Cotton Mills in Interwar Mumbai' on JSTOR, www.jstor.org, n.d., https://doi.org/10.2307/40276443.

By this time, Hari Prasad Solanki had introduced Champakbhai to his good friend, Suryakant Chandulal Dani, whom I referred to earlier. Dani and Choksey—born in the same year and hence of the same age—immediately hit it off, and the three of them—Hari Prasad, Champakbhai and Suryakantbhai—grew to be very close as young men setting up their careers in Mumbai in the early and mid-1930s. Champakbhai and Suryakantbhai's friendship lies at the very heart and origin of Asian Paints and this story unfolds by chance, not choice.

A Fallout in the Family

In 1936, Champakbhai fell out with his family and chose to leave home. While he would heal relations later, this phase was particularly acrimonious. Champakbhai told his sister, 'I will stay on the footpath, but I will never return to this house.'

Champakbhai was upset after this fallout and, as per family records, one day he spent time wandering around on the streets in Girgaum before landing up at Suryakantbhai's house in the afternoon. Since Suryakantbhai was at work, an emotionally distraught Champakbhai poured out his story to Kantaben, Suryakantbhai's wife. Kantaben patiently listened to the outburst, calmed him down, and offered him advice, support and words of courage at this sensitive moment; something that Champakbhai would remember for the rest of his life.

The Choksey family recalled to me that family relations between Hiralal and Champakbhai were strained at this point, and after leaving his home Champakbhai slept on benches at Chowpatty Beach and also stayed with Suryakantbhai for a brief while before finding accommodation for himself. As time went by, the three friends would settle down in their respective jobs—Champakbhai as a cotton jobber, Suryakantbhai in a pharmacy and Solanki as a typist.

The Birth of a Trading Agency

A few years later, Suryakantbhai was offered an agency to sell paints made by a local manufacturer, Pranjeevandas Vasani. To start this business, Suryakantbhai began looking for a partner and approached Champakbhai. But Champakbhai was busy with his job and passed on the opportunity to Solanki. Solanki did not have the risk appetite to leave his job for a new venture and requested Champakbhai to reconsider.

This seemingly innocuous moment in time was when Asian Paints was born. It is not known what exactly drove Champakbhai to change his mind and decide to quit his career as a jobber and leap into business. He was very familiar with risk and gambling, given that he played cards during Janmashtami and speculated in the stock and commodities markets in that era. It is possible that he decided to bet on his good friend's offer.

Whatever the reason, this was the last time Champakbhai made a switch in his career. His ability and willingness to take risks made him quit being a cotton jobber (a profession that, it turned out, would die out in the next few decades) and start a paints agency with Suryakantbhai. The two young men's friendship turned into a partnership. On the auspicious day of Dussehra in 1939, Champakbhai and Suryakantbhai started their paints agency, calling it Neptune Trading Agency, a possible inspiration from Vasani's company which was called Venus Paint Works.

The agency did so well that it soon became one of Vasani's largest agents. The war provided a ready demand for domestic paints but Champakbhai and Suryakantbhai had a natural flair for enrolling customers, getting repeat business from them, and establishing trust with their customers. As per one record, the duo had a list of 130 shopkeepers on their list within Mumbai.

Over time, however, the biggest constraint would not be demand but quality. The partners noticed that customers were complaining of poor quality, and this was impacting sales. They tried to convince Vasani to improve the quality of his paints but without the knowledge or possession of skills or the right machinery, Vasani could not do this. All their pleas fell on deaf ears. Vasani had also dangled the carrot of partnership in his firm with Champakbhai and Suryakantbhai but despite becoming one of his largest agents, this offer never came to fruition.

Champakbhai and Suryakantbhai were left with no choice. The only way to improve the quality of paints, meet the rising demand, and be in control of their sales was to manufacture paints on their own.

After yet another year of not realizing their dreams, Champakbhai and Suryakantbhai decided to leave Vasani and start their own manufacturing facility. To fund this idea, both of them looked for partners and found two: Chimanlal Choksi (Choksi spelt with an 'i' and not related to Champakbhai whose surname was Choksey spelt with an 'ey') and Suryakantbhai's brother-in-law, Arvind Vakil.

Thus, four partners came together, and on 1 February 1942, they rented a garage on Jairajbhai Street, Foras Road and began the manufacturing unit. Incidentally, this was the era when trams operated in Bombay and the Asian Paints factory in Foras Road was located near Tram Line 13. Suryakantbhai and Champakbhai knew how to sell paint but neither they nor the new partners knew how to manufacture it. To start with, they hired a few workers and went back to the basic principle of primary colours (red, blue and yellow) and creating other colours by mixing them.

The production facility was very primitive with all the raw materials, pigments and oils being physically stamped and pounded by workers to produce colour. They had to make one product—anti-corrosive paints for ships, or paints that would rustproof the parts of ships made of iron and steel. Hence, the primary products made by this factory were red lead paint, zinc paste and the paint colour known as Battleship Grey. They also purchased linseed oil and varnish in bulk to resell them as well as use them for making the paints.

Just like World War I, imports were stopped in World War II as well. The supply of paints in Mumbai was, therefore, severely disrupted. There were large local manufacturers of paint in Mumbai—like Gahagan Paints (later Kansai Nerolac) in Lower Parel, but there was enough unmet demand. Ships coming into Mumbai hunted around for paint for their vessels. Ship painting was done by specialized firms, and one such firm, Hyderali Ismyljee was looking for a large supply of red paint. As luck would have it, Champakbhai learnt of this and convinced Hyderali to purchase the entire order from them. The factory remained open all night to meet the large order. After this, Hyderali became a regular client. Ships became big business for the partners during World War II.

One story narrated by Champakbhai to employees was when they approached a ship chandler asking for an increase in prices for their red lead paint since that paint received no complaints from the ships. The chandler told Champakbhai, 'You are not getting any complaints because those ships never made it to the shore. They were shot down and sunk mid-sea.'

To recap, this was Champakbhai Choksey at the age of twenty-six. He was schooled in English, friendly with people, aggressive with bullies, and worked in at least two jobs—first, the watch company and then as a cotton jobber. His best friends were Suryakant Dani and Hari Prasad Solanki, and he was one of four partners in a firm, manufacturing paints. The year was 1942, and Champakbhai's story had just begun.

Author's note: An appendix on the paints industry is given in this book. Reading it is essential to understanding how competitive dynamics unfolded for the four partners.

Chapter 2

From Trading to Manufacturing

'The strength of a woman is not measured by the impact that all her hardships in life have had on her, but the strength of a woman is measured by the extent of her refusal to allow those hardships to dictate her and who she becomes.'

—*C. JoyBell*

India's struggle for freedom moved forward in the 1940s, culminating in independence in 1947. Its economy was still dominated by the British but large Indian business houses like the Tatas, Birlas, Dalmias and Walchands (Doshi) were slowly expanding their empire across commodities from steel to textiles to shipping, as well as in banking. Paints companies, mainly foreign, were setting up and expanding operations, giving Asian Paints their first competitors. In this era, industrial paints (used for ships, buildings, etc.) were the dominant market for paints. Thus, these were the times when Asian Paints was born.

With the demand from World War II continuing to drive sales, the partners increased their range of products and were looking to expand beyond Mumbai as well. However, this time around they ran into a familiar obstacle—a lack of capital to expand. In times of war, supply had to be uninterrupted even as incoming payments were unpredictable and often involved long periods of credit. The operations were not yet self-sustaining.

This cash crunch was alleviated by an acquaintance, Jamnadas Vora, who lent them money after they set up the initial partnership. With these funds, the partners had room to breathe in terms of liquidity as well as funds for capital expenditure for buying machinery. Jamnadas Vora was also inducted as the fifth partner, given his capital contribution. The partnership needed a name, and the responsibility of naming the new company fell to Suryakantbhai who, as the story goes, took the suggestion of a friend, opened a phone directory and chose a name at random. That name was Asian Oil and Paint Company. Champakbhai and Suryakantbhai started Neptune Trading Agency on the Dussehra of that year. In a similar auspicious moment, the Asian Oil and Paint Company was started on the Hindu New Year on 9 November 1942.

With the problems around space and capital resolved, the partners kept growing the business. The demand driven by World War II began to wane as the war neared its end in 1945, but luckily for the partners, their business had now expanded enough to sustain itself beyond World War II-led demand. By 1945, they needed more space and took up a small factory in Girgaum belonging to another seth.

On the advice of their chartered accountant, the partnership was converted into a private limited company called Asian Oil and Paint Co. (India) Limited, incorporated on 24 October 1945. Jamnadas Vora was still part of the company then. As per the Asian Paints Memorandum and Articles of Association, this was the original list of signatories who signed when the private limited company acquired the partnership.

Table 2.1 is an extract from the Memorandum and Articles of Association of Asian Paints and not an ownership schedule of the original partnership that started in 1942 and was converted into a private limited company in 1945. Notwithstanding that, from this table, it appears that at least in terms of the number of shares, the Vora family (Jamnadas, his wife Jayabai and his son Himatlal) held 36 per cent in the partnership, versus 64 per cent with the original four founding families.

Table 2.1: List of partners of Asian Oil and Paint Company (India) in 1945

	Name	Number of shares
1	Suryakant Chandulal Dani	160 shares of Rs 100 each
2	Champaklal Hiralal Choksey	160 shares of Rs 100 each
3	Arvind Ishwarlal Vakil	160 shares of Rs 100 each
4	Jamnadas Vithaldas Vora	200 shares of Rs 100 each
5	Himatlal Jamnadas Vora	110 shares of Rs 100 each
6	Chimanlal Nanabhai Choksi	160 shares of Rs 100 each
7	Jayabai Jamnadas Vora	50 shares of Rs 100 each

(Source: Asian Paints Memorandum and Articles of Association[1])

The Voras' capital was important to the original four partners, but the Voras did not stay for too long. One account from the Chokseys indicates that the Voras fell into financial trouble, sold their stake to the original four families in 1948, and exited the company. Their decision to sell is something that only fate can pass a verdict on.

In 1965, the partners changed the name to Asian Paints (India) Private Limited since the company stopped selling oils. In 1973, the company became a 'deemed' public company[2] and its name was changed to Asian Paints (India) Limited although public participation in the form of equity shares happened only in 1982. In 2005, the name was changed to Asian Paints Limited to reflect the global ambitions[3] of the company.

---

[1] Asian Paints website, https://www.asianpaints.com/content/dam/asianpaints/website/secondary-navigation/investors/MOA/AsianPaintsLimited_Memorandum&ArticlesofAssociation.pdf, accessed 7 January 2024.

[2] A hybrid between a public and a private company, as per the old Companies Act, 1956, this concept was laid to rest in the year 2000. Further reading: Lalit Kumar, 'Deemed Companies Laid to Rest', (2011), https://economictimes.indiatimes.com/policy/deemed-companies-laid-to-rest/articleshow/10525588.cms

[3] Asian Paints annual report, 2005–06, p. 27.

Even as World War II ended, Asian Paints' growth continued unabated. By the mid-1940s, they needed more land and capital. This time around, the partners wanted to upgrade from makeshift facilities and garages to a larger dedicated plot of land. Enter Manilal Gandhi who owned a plot in Matunga (about 10 km north of Bhuleshwar). He was willing to give it at a reasonable rent to the company. The agreement was signed in 1947 but not without some challenges.

I met Jayant Gandhi, son of Manilal Gandhi, who owned the Matunga plot. Gandhi has conducted multiple businesses from corrugated boxes to producing the superhit play, *Bottoms Up*. He even recalled Himatlal Vora when we spoke about the early days of the partnership. He told me:

> 'We had a big property in Matunga that we had given to a person to manage. As time went by, this person refused to leave. Himatlal Vora vouched for Asian Paints and on his word, I gave them the property. Asian Paints helped us with the person occupying our property, and that's why we leased the property to them. I became a good friend of the families.
>
> 'They often told me stories of how they used to go door to door selling paints, in the old days. I traded in shares and hence would often go to the stock exchange (PJ Towers, Dalal Street in South Mumbai). Their old office was situated in Das Chambers, which is close to the exchange. Hence, I met Champakbhai often and learnt a lot from him.
>
> 'One day he called me to his office and asked, "Jayant what car do you drive?" I told him a Morris Minor. Lo and behold, after a few weeks, he called me to his house and gave me the keys to Ashvinaben's Fiat car which was in pristine condition! He told me to pay whatever I thought was the right price for the car. He was that kind of person—very charismatic and flamboyant. Suryakantbhai was the firm, grounded and rooted person and Champakbhai was the high-flyer. That's why their combination worked so well.'

With the manufacturing shifted to Matunga, the Girgaum facility became an office. As the business grew, the office would shift to Das Chambers near the Bombay Stock Exchange and then to Nirmal Building, Nariman Point. The Matunga facility lasted for a decade for the firm, and as the business continued to grow, the partners branched out of Mumbai by appointing agents in Maharashtra (Nagpur), Gujarat (Bhavnagar, Rajakot), Madhya Pradesh (Indore) and the south (Madras, Secunderabad), with varying degrees of success.

Industry Dynamics

The paints industry played an important part in Champakbhai's life. Among the original four partners, it was Champakbhai who led Asian Paints when it came to industry matters. He got along very well with the leaders of competitions and never let business rivalry affect his relationships. This is why, even today, he is remembered as a statesman of the industry. While I have given a primer on the paints industry in the appendix, what follows next is a discussion on the competitive dynamics in the 1950s and 1960s.

Champakbhai—Early History in Paints Associations

By the time Asian Paints shifted to Matunga, the company was growing in size, as was the paints industry. There were two key features of the paints industry in that era. First, the industry was based almost entirely in Calcutta and second, the large players, such as Goodlass Nerolac, Jenson & Nicholson and Hadfields (later Berger Paints) in the industry were mainly foreign-owned and foreign-run organizations. This was to be expected since Calcutta in the 1930s and 1940s was at the peak[4] of its

[4] Amol Agrawal, 'When Bombay Overtook Calcutta: A History of India's Financial Geography', *Mint*, 24 June 2017, https://www.livemint.com/Sundayapp/Z8DStEXICwm3MFvlE7PFXI/When-Bombay-overtook-Calcutta-A-history-of-Indias-financia.html.

prominence as a financial centre. Thanks to the ports in Calcutta, trade volumes and the banking business were higher (the East India Company established joint stock banking in Calcutta in 1806 and in Bombay in 1840) and therefore more companies were floated in Calcutta than in Bombay in that era.

Dominated by British-owned paints companies, the paints industry united in Calcutta to form the Association of Paint, Colour and Varnish Manufacturers Association in India (APCVMI) in 1937. But in a few years, a very young and motivated Indian entrepreneur, Prahlad Chandra Chanda entered the association strongly in favour of Indian manufacturers. Thus, there became two separate bodies, one with British owners (Paint Federation) and another with Indian owners (IPMA or Indian Paint Manufacturers Association) in 1941.

Chanda was senior to Champakbhai, and both the senior paints owners had a long-abiding admiration for each other—another hallmark of Champakbhai's way of doing things—he took competition seriously in business, but outside of that, he was on very friendly terms with almost all his contemporaries in competing businesses.

In a famous and oft-told story of when Asian Paints was still a small company, Champakbhai had visited a paint dealer's shop in Null Bazar (a busy, crowded market area in Mumbai) only to be promptly thrown out, much to his chagrin, to make way for 'the Sahib', Scarlett of Goodlass Wall, a British paints company. Champakbhai never forgot the incident and repeated it to his family and employees alike; the family version goes that Champakbhai angrily (and prophetically) retorted to the shop owner that there will come a day in the future when he (the shop owner) would throw 'the Sahib' out to make way for Champakbhai.

Notwithstanding that, Champakbhai would become friends with Scarlett, a friendship that paved the way for the merger of the federation and IPMA in 1960. In fact, it was Scarlett who convinced Champakbhai to join the federation, something that Champakbhai did very reluctantly; the added benefit was the occasional insight into how the Europeans managed their operations with talented professionals—a very different way of functioning from the Indian family business which relied on family, friends and community. Maybe Champakbhai's tenure in the federation was useful in formulating the idea of hiring professionals in key positions. Eventually, Champakbhai switched sides and joined IPMA in 1958.

The federation and IPMA merged post-Independence—with the efforts of P.C. Chanda—in 1960 to form the Indian Paints Association (IPA), India's foremost industry body representing paints companies across the country. Chairpersons of the IPA are usually leaders of the paints industry, from the first president (quite obviously, P.C. Chanda) to the current president, Ashok Gupta of Shalimar Paints. P.C. Chanda was the founder of Chanda Paints, founded in 1932, which exists even today[5] and is a leading manufacturer of industrial coatings in India.

Competitive Scenario in the 1950s

Asian Paints was making the transition from a small manufacturing unit to a large paints company. Its competition, hence, was from both sides. At the top end were the paints companies in Calcutta, namely the foreign brands set up in the 1920s such as Shalimar Paints (the first paints factory in India), ICI, Jenson & Nicholson and British Paints. In Bombay, the major paints companies were Goodlass Wall (from the Gahagan paints factory) and Blundell Eomite (from the Elephant Oil Mills factory). The unorganized sector dominated the middle and lower ends of the paints industry.

Between the industrial and decorative segments, industrial was larger in that era given that the government was among the biggest consumers. The largest selling single product[6] for a long time in the paints industry was premium gloss, which

[5] Chanda Paints, http://www.chandapaints.com/, accessed on 9 January 2024.

[6] Biji Kurien, *Half a Century and Still at the Crease*, Productivity & Quality Publishing Private Limited, 2021.

accounted for nearly 30–40 per cent of all the paints sold in terms of value and volume at one time. Premium gloss was used across applications such as outdoor hoardings, billboards, signboards and household uses such as doors, windows, grills and gates. In the wall coatings market, paste distemper was the largest selling interior paint and white cement paint was the largest selling exterior paint.

The Importance of Ownership

Besides being foreign-owned, Asian Paints' competition would go on to see frequent changes in ownership. In contrast, Asian Paints was both home-grown and has the original promoters (except the Chokseys) even today. This is an important point to flesh out here because it shows how key the friendship of the first generation was in the early days of the company. In a ruthlessly competitive and complicated industry like paints, seeing your owners change frequently can demoralize even the most motivated professional CEO who will worry about his prospects under new owners.

Almost all paints companies that started in the 1920s and 1930s went through changes in ownership, due to reasons such as the foreign-majority shareholder merging globally (ICI and AkzoNobel) or the Indian government mandating foreign owners to reduce their stake (FERA regulation in 1973), etc. Change in ownership can have a major impact on the fortunes of any company. Here are two case studies:

Shalimar Paints

Take India's first paints factory—Shalimar Paints—which has seen three changes in its 120+-year history. The first change in ownership was in 1928 when it passed from Turner and Wright to Pinchin Johnson & Associates (UK). The second change took it to International Paints in 1964, after it became a public limited company in 1961. By 1973, when Indian regulation (under the Foreign Exchange and Regulation Act, 1973) was clamping down on foreign-owned companies, International Paints came under its radar and the foreign owners had to bring down their shareholding in favour of Indian shareholders. The company also lost focus and began slipping.

In 1989, in the third and last change, Shalimar Paints went to Indian owners (O.P. Jindal Group and S.S. Jhunjhunwala Group). By this time, Shalimar Paints, the largest paints company in the 1960s, had already been overtaken by Asian Paints, Berger Paints and Kansai Nerolac. For a company that prides itself on painting Howrah Bridge and Rashtrapati Bhavan, it had to shutter[7] its century-old plant in the 2010s as it became unviable, even though the Jindal (JSW) Group entered the paints industry (with its JSW Paints) in 2019.

Berger Paints

Berger Paints, on the other hand, is a success story of sorts with committed promoters transforming a company. But the origin story of Berger Paints has three different threads that came together only in 1991. In the first thread, Lewis Berger started making paints in 1760 in Germany as a young colour chemist. His sons converted his business into a company which merged internationally with Jenson & Nicholson in 1960, to form Berger, Jenson & Nicholson (BJN).

In the second thread, Hadfields (as shown in Table A2, Section 4, Appendix 1) began operations in India in 1923 and was acquired by British Paints in 1947. Celanese Corporation acquired British Paints in 1965. These two threads merged when BJN UK acquired British Paints from Celanese Corporation in

[7] Sambit Saha, 'Jindals Add Colour to Palette', *Telegraph India*, 24 August 2018, https://www.telegraphindia.com/business/jindals-add-colour-to-palette/cid/1457244.

1969, thus becoming the second-largest paints company in the world after ICI's paints division.

But in 1970, BJN UK was acquired by then German conglomerate Hoechst AG, thus bringing Lewis Berger back home to Germany. Hoechst AG was also in India in the pharmaceuticals business, in association with the United Breweries (UB) Group, headed by liquor baron Vittal Mallya, father of Vijay Mallya. The Mallyas, thus, renamed British Paints as Berger Paints in India. Finally, the third thread features the Dhingra brothers, Kuldip Singh Dhingra and Gurbachan Singh Dhingra, who are fourth-generation entrepreneurs in the paints industry.

Their family had modest but deep beginnings in paint shops and factories in Amritsar and Delhi. The Dhingra brothers continued the tradition, despite major family upheavals, and became large exporters of paint to Russia in the 1980s. By the 1990s, they were looking to diversify away from exports. This is when the Mallyas sold Berger Paints to the Dhingra brothers in 1991, merging all the threads. After the Dhingras acquired Berger Paints, they worked hard at transforming the company and made it India's second-largest paints manufacturer, a huge improvement from number seven in 1980.[8]

The Critical Role of Women and Family in Champakbhai's Life

Even as Asian Paints expanded to Matunga, Champakbhai's personal life went through major turmoil through the 1940s and the 1950s. He got married in 1940 at the age of twenty-four to Kumudben Chhowalla who had a large family, including three sisters—Sushilaben, Ashvinaben and Hansaben—and two brothers, Jaykumarbhai and Pravinbhai. Champakbhai and Kumudben had two children, their son Girish (born in 1942,

[8] Saurabh Mukherjea, *The Unusual Billionaires* (2016).

when Asian Paints started as a partnership) and daughter Rita (1944). Unfortunately, Kumudben passed away in 1946. This was almost a replay of Champakbhai's father's life—he too had lost his wife early on.

Girish Choksey, the eldest of the second generation of the Choksey family, told me, 'I was four and a half years old and I remember seeing my father sitting on the footpath and crying.' Having felt the love and support of his mother in his early years, Champakbhai wanted the same for his children. This is when he reached out to Sushilaben to take care of Girish and Rita. Sushilaben, who stayed in Surat, had been married to Champakbhai's uncle and had been widowed at a very young age. Since Kumudben was Sushilaben's sister, Champakbhai made an emotional request to their family to let Sushilaben relocate to Mumbai and raise her sister's children in the same way that his eldest sister, Padmaben, had helped raise him.

Sushilaben agreed and moved to Mumbai to live with the Choksey family and help raise Girish and Rita. Champakbhai's story cannot be written without mentioning Sushilaben. She was central to bringing stability to Champakbhai's family life when he was thirty years old. At this point in time, the Choksey family lived at the Sonawala Building in Tardeo, a large colony of many buildings situated less than two km from Mumbai Central Railway Terminal in South Mumbai.

After that, Champakbhai made another, more audacious request. He wanted to remarry and he requested Ashvinaben, Kumudben's younger sister to be his wife. There was uproar in Champakbhai's family. Initially, Ashvinaben was reluctant since Champakbhai was many years her senior. It took a long time to convince her, and finally in 1947, the same year as Asian Paints shifted to their Matunga factory, Champakbhai and Ashvinaben got married. As Champakbhai's family did not approve of the match, they did not attend his wedding and broke off all ties with him at this point. Champakbhai and Ashvinaben had two sons—Atul Choksey (1951) and Amit Choksey (1954).

By the time he was thirty-eight years old, Champakbhai finally had a semblance of stability in his family, although the initial turmoil never stopped him from keeping his attention focused on Asian Paints. 'The Sonawala Building was near the old factory and any time there was any problem, Papa would rush to the factory. There were times when he would stand alone on the balcony of our house late into the night, thinking about Asian Paints and its future. Asian Paints was his life,' Girish told me. To give him that much space to think about Asian Paints, the presence of Sushilaben and Ashvinaben was critical to Champakbhai. 'Without their support, Papa would not be what he was,' Parul Choksey, Atul's wife, told me emphatically.

After Atul was born, Champakbhai reconciled with his family. Frayed relationships were healed and Champakbhai did everything he could to ensure that both families were taken care of, from jobs at Asian Paints to dealerships to contracting work—he did whatever it took. Once relations were back to normal, he would hire a truck and take all the children and his relatives out on Republic Day (26 January) to see the city lit up for the occasion. Champakbhai did all of this alongside planning the next phase of expansion at Asian Paints with his partners. For all practical purposes, Sushilaben and Ashvinaben were the foundations of the Choksey family.

As for Sushilaben, she stayed with the Chokseys for the rest of her life. Parul said, 'Till she died, Sushilaben was lovingly called Rang Wali Ba. She used to go to the Sadhubella Temple, near Mahalaxmi Temple every day and once she found that the paint on the temple had worn off. She told Papa (Champakbhai) to have it painted and Papa made sure that the temple got a fresh coat of paint every year.'

The role of women was so central and definitive in Champakbhai's life that he went out of his way to ensure their independence. For example, he insisted that each of his three daughters-in-law learn how to drive and drive their cars. This came in handy during an anecdote narrated to me by the family.

Amit Choksey was the rebel of Champakbhai's four children. At the age of sixteen, a very young and mischievous Amit took a parachute firecracker (you lit the parachute, which would leap up and then float down as a small chute unfolded) opened it up, threw the chute and lit the gunpowder with a matchstick. The flame exploded and burnt his face and he had to be rushed to hospital. The only problem? No one was at home and Sunita, Girish's wife, had to drive the car. But she was from Ahmedabad, and had only recently married Girish and learnt to drive. She didn't know her way around the narrow and complicated roads of Tardeo. So Amit, with his face burning in pain, told her the route to Harkisondas Hospital, where they went first. When he came to know about the incident, Champakbhai rushed to the hospital and on their doctor's advice moved Amit to Bhatia Hospital which had a reputed ward for burns. Amit was in hospital for a few days and recovered fully.

Another example that I was told was that Ashvinaben and her sister-in-law ran the canteen at the Asian Paints office at Nirmal Building, Nariman Point and their food—especially the Gujarati thali—was very popular with the staff.

Champakbhai was liberal with his children and indulged them in their passions. Amit, for example, raced cars and bikes professionally when he was young. In his racing career, by his count, he had seventeen accidents on motorcycles, scooters and cars, including falling 30 feet at a rally. 'Papa gave me the liberty to ride cars and motorcycles. He dealt with my accidents well and I really respect him for that. I did everything—car racing, Monsoon Rally, Himalayan Rally, taking my cars on the plane from home to racing circuits. I had a lot of adventures before finally settling down,' Amit told me. Amit worked at Asian Paints in the mid-1970s and currently owns and runs Mazda Colours. He is also the consul to the Slovak Republic in India.

'Live with dignity, never be dependent on your children or anyone else, have a house and bank balance of your own till you are alive—these were some lessons we learnt from him,' Parul told me. Thus, Ashvinaben owned a home and was fully in charge of her finances, and the tradition followed in the next generation with Sunita, Parul and Priti. Champakbhai also believed in higher education and encouraged the wives of his three sons to continue their education even after marriage—contrary to the beliefs of conservative Gujarati families in that era. 'He went to Mumbai University and got the forms for me to pursue an MA (master in arts) in psychology,' Parul told me. Similarly, he insisted to Priti's parents that Priti complete her graduation even though she was getting married to Amit.

Champakbhai was also open about his investment beliefs with the family. 'He believed in spreading his investments across different assets—over and above his biggest investment (in Asian Paints). He believed in real estate but only in our own individual name not hidden inside a company. Of course, he believed in buying your own home and keeping it on your own name. He also believed in gold and silver and when he bought these in bulk, we [when we were young] used to wonder why he was doing that,' Parul told me.

Champakbhai was a very keen observer and learnt from the splits in large business families, some of which played out publicly and some that remained in the realm of rumours. He was a very strong believer in families staying together in harmony and also in discipline. *The Godfather* was his favourite book and like many who loved the film, he spoke of his favourite scenes with his family. Prashant Choksey, Girish's second son and Champakbhai's second grandson recalls, 'He told me to watch *The Godfather*, in particular the scene where Santino "Sonny" Corleone speaks out of turn at the meeting between his father Don Corleone and competitor, Virgil Sollozzo, on the drug trade. Dadaji told me that when you come into a meeting, you never counter your own family.'

From very early on, Champakbhai believed in transparency and openness within the family. Once every month, he would have a meeting with all three sons and their wives to discuss any issues at home that they wanted to talk about. Daily, the dinner table at home was the chosen spot for all three generations of the family to meet and bond, as we will explore further in Chapter 5. Everyone had dinner together every evening at home and matters were discussed openly and freely. Right down to discussing and preparing his will with his family, Champakbhai believed in transparency. And 'family' was not restricted to Champakbhai's family by blood. Champakbhai saw his partners as his family too, and the feeling was mutual between Suryakantbhai, Chimanbhai and Arvindbhai. All four families—Chokseys, Danis, Choksis and Vakils, have warm and cordial relations. Even today, the Chokseys and Vakils stay in the same building, Geetanjali, while the Choksis and Danis stay nearby in South Mumbai. Diwali would be celebrated together and the children of all four partners got along very well. Family was everything to Champakbhai and as we will see later, even his employees were as good as his family. Champakbhai even took care of the support staff at his home and, in some cases, even provided for them in his will. 'He believed in looking after people who looked after us and made our lives easy. We learnt this from him and continue it even today,' Parul told me.

Part 2

Breaking All the Rules

Chapter 3

Kitchen Relationships

'Coming together is a beginning, staying together is progress, and working together is success.'

—Henry Ford

Asian Paints took merely twenty-five years to become India's largest paints manufacturer. From 1942 to 1967, there were a handful of key decisions that transformed it from a small-time paints manufacturer to an industry leader. In this chapter, we will look at three such decisions that defied paints industry (and family business) practices in that era—identifying gaps ignored by the paints makers, going mass market with a network of dealers and establishing deep relations with them and finally, hiring talent from outside the family and friends network. In the next chapter, we look at hiring chemists and strengthening the bench of non-family professionals.

Findings Gaps in the Market

When Asian Paints started, the paints industry in India was primarily led by the industrial segment and dominated by foreign companies. The decorative segment was largely urban, and for households, the choice was between cheap paint made by local, unorganized manufacturers and expensive emulsions made by foreign companies. Champakbhai and the founders thus noticed significant gaps in the system. Here are two examples made famous in Saurabh Mukherjea's *The Unusual Billionaires*.

Example 1: Smaller Tins

Festivals have always been a big demand driver for paints, and in rural areas, during festivals like Pongal (Tamil Nadu) and Pola (Maharashtra), villagers paint the horns of their bulls with bright colours like red and yellow. Similarly, the bottom panels of the front doors of homes in Tamil Nadu have small stripes also painted in red and yellow, which are considered auspicious colours.

Saurabh Mukherjea, in *The Unusual Billionaires*, quotes a former employee of Asian Paints as saying, 'Champakbhai used to say that "*Gareeb apni dahleej zaroor rang karega, poora ghar chahe na kare* [a poor household will always colour its entrance door even if they do not paint the rest of the house]."' But in both these examples, the requirement is for limited quantities of high-quality (say, for the bulls to withstand mud and marsh) paint for this purpose, and Asian Paints delivered these to them in small tins of 50 ml and 100 ml. This was among the earliest breakthroughs.

Example 2: Connecting with the Masses

Before paints became household products, they were luxuries beyond the reach of the majority of people. So, if you're wondering how the masses painted their homes, here is Kuldip Singh Dhingra explaining the process to Sonu Bhasin:

> 'When people had to paint their house in the 1960s, they would go to the shop and buy *safeda* (white, stiff paint), varnish, double boiled linseed oil and turpentine separately. The white paint was the base pigment, made usually of either zinc oxide or titanium dioxide. The varnish was the binder, or the resin, and the turpentine was the solvent. People would buy drums and cans of each and the kaarigars would mix them to create paint. For colour, they would buy cans of

paste pigment or paste colour and mix it into the white paint mixture. Voila! The paint was ready.'

A step above safeda was a wide variety of distempers, ranging from cheap to expensive. Asian Paints' 'Tractor Distemper' was placed above cheap and basic distemper (low-quality paint that would peel off soon, stick to clothes and stink) and below expensive plastic emulsion paints made by foreign competition (such as Robbialac from Jenson & Nicholson).

Tractor connected well with a vast majority of people in the semi-urban and rural markets given that agriculture was a major activity in that era. Alongside Tractor paste distemper, Asian Paints had Three Mangoes, a medium-quality gloss (used on doors, windows, gates, grills, etc.) which was also named to connect with the masses. As Biji Kurien, who was in charge of the Madras branch in the late 1960s and the early 1970s, writes in his book, *Half a Century and Still at the Crease: A Journey through 50-plus Years of a Management Professional*, 'The brand name had registered well with the retailers and painters, who influenced the purchase of paints considerably those days. So much so, the company was referred to as the "Mango Company" and the manager and salesmen were referred to as the "Mango company manager and salesmen".'

In 1959, Gattu was launched (as we discuss in Chapter 11 on advertising), a mascot that connected well with the rural and semi-urban markets.

Everything Everywhere All at Once

When Asian Paints started, the term 'supply chain' didn't exist. If the paints industry was dominated by foreign brands, then their distribution would be dominated by a bunch of large distributors including those who were exclusive to a company. Small shopkeepers and mom-and-pop stores were the last mile who had to buy from these large distributors who were also free to set up their shops. These large distributors enjoyed considerable power and clout and were treated well by the foreign companies with liberal terms of payment credit, at times extending to a year, payable on Diwali.

These distributors[1] had neither the compulsion nor the motivation to invest in distribution infrastructure. They did not move out to semi-urban and rural areas. Distributors protected their turf well, making it tough for a new distributor or even a new paint company to break in. The system worked well for everyone except the small retailer who was beholden to the larger distributor. In the beginning, Champakbhai went along with this system. Having been kicked out by a large distributor in Mumbai, he knew that while large distributors would not care about a small Indian company, he also could not afford to ignore them. His stronghold was Bombay and Maharashtra, and his products were doing well in these markets; Asian Paints' first dealership was in Sangli, south Maharashtra.

But Champakbhai loved autonomy and did not want to depend on anyone. He knew that this system restricted a larger footprint for Asian Paints. The founders had been to the villages and saw how the system worked against the smaller shops. Atul Choksey told me, 'In those days, Champakbhai had a vision to sell in every village. He saw that villagers then had a real problem of non-availability of paint in the right quality and quantity and that the competition was not serving them at all.'

The Open Market Policy

So, Asian Paints moved to an open-door retail dealer policy or open market policy. They decided to sell to literally anyone—big or small, exclusive or non-exclusive—who could pay within their credit period. As Ramaswamy and Namakumari write,

> 'AP (Asian Paints) established a large chain of company-operated depots/stock points throughout its vast marketing

[1] Mini case 16.1 on Asian Paints in Marketing Management 6e by V.S. Ramaswamy and S. Namakumari (2018).

> territory, from where the retail dealers could conveniently pick up their requirements. AP's basic strategies necessitated a large network of stock points/depots. And the depots had to be company-operated. AP did not have any wholesale distributors to shoulder the responsibility of operating the stock points.'

As P.M. Murty told me, 'That was a very tough decision to make. There would have been some initial losses but that (decision) provided you the opportunity to ensure that your network is broadened. Once you have got over the initial hump, you are no longer in the clutches of any of the large distributors.' So, Asian Paints significantly ramped up their distribution to go directly to the shopkeepers. This disruption affected the large distributors who did not take too well, initially, to Asian Paints' decision.

Atul Choksey told me,

> 'We could see that demand in rural and semi-urban areas was high. So, we opened stocking points there to service the smaller dealers better. It worked very well. Obviously, the big distributors weren't happy. So, Champakbhai and Suryakantbhai, who always openly welcomed all dealers, called them to Bombay. I remember around five to seven of them, some from Bombay, some from Pune and Aurangabad landed at our office. They said, "We built your brand, your product, your business over time and now you are taking it away from us!"'

Champakbhai and Suryakantbhai told them, 'Here is our promise. Your business will not go down even by Re 1 because of what we are doing. If it goes down because of your issues, then you have to look into that. But we guarantee you that it will only increase even if smaller shops stop buying from you—and they will stop buying from you. If it still goes down, meet us here at the end of the year.'

'They did not return at the end of the year,' Atul Choksey told me, adding, 'and this was the message to all the dealers across the country.'

Atul Choksey gave a specific example of a very large and very tough dealer in Dadar, one of the busiest and most crowded areas in Mumbai. Champakbhai and Suryakantbhai told him, 'Do not think that we will do this only in rural areas. We will open additional dealers in Dadar. I want one paint dealer in every lane. Why should you say there will be no other dealer in Dadar? We want more dealers. And my promise to you is that your business will not go down.' That is how the entire market was opened up by Asian Paints to any dealer—large or small—who was willing to pay within the terms of credit.

And once the small retail network grew large enough, Asian Paints became too big to be ignored by the large distributors in other parts of India who had avoided them till then. Biji Kurien called[2] it 'Muhammed Ghazni tactics' of attacking Delhi—namely, the company targeted the centre of power after capturing the outlying areas.

Deepening Dealer Relations

Going rural and selling in smaller quantities was the easier part. A new entrant could copy that. The tougher part was building personal, one-on-one relations with the dealers, especially the smaller ones. This took decades to build and paid off in ways even the founders could not imagine—a moat was slowly created that stands strong even today.

It started with the founders meeting smaller retailers and shopkeepers in smaller towns and in villages, who loved talking to the owners of a company who gave them the time of day and treated them like they would treat guests or even relatives at home—and Gujaratis are known for their hospitality. Contrast this with the foreign paints companies where small shopkeepers would be at the mercy of large distributors, and even if a foreign

[2] Biji Kurien, *Half a Century and Counting*.

boss visited their shop, he would come with an entourage and protocols, distinctly giving off a whiff of the colonial era.

Slowly and surely, Asian Paints built a large base of retailers, shopkeepers and dealers who would happily stock and supply their product. Suryakantbhai was a legend in building these relationships. The culture would go on to become so ingrained within the company that it would eventually be called kitchen relationships. Suryakantbhai did this so well that even as the company grew, he would personally be in touch with dealers. When the dealers visited their Mumbai office, Suryakantbhai ensured that the dealers and their families were given a tour of Mumbai, their kids given gifts, and the dealer's every need was taken care of, personally.

Over the years, this culture would eventually seep across the organization and become part of the DNA. For example, in 1969 when Biji Kurien headed the Madras branch, he accompanied salesmen by car instead of public transport so they could chart their own route. They travelled the length and breadth of the then-Madras state, meeting dealers face to face, and Biji, who was also fluent in Tamil, gained the trust and confidence of the smaller retailers.

The backbone of Asian Paints' success was the dealers, and this chapter describes only the beginning. As we go further, we will see how the computer helped improve deliveries and how the tinting machines made stocking easier. No wonder dealers hold Asian Paints in high regard. Many ex-employees of Asian Paints are still in touch with these dealers, even today. Here are examples of kitchen relationships narrated to me in my interviews:

1. K.B.S. Anand—'The Scariest Incident in My Life'

K.B.S. Anand, a mechanical engineer from IIT Bombay and a postgraduate diploma in management (PGDM) holder from IIM Calcutta (IIMC), joined Asian Paints in 1979 and retired in 2020 as managing director and chief executive officer.

Anand told me that his most dangerous task was not when he was in the Kasna (Uttar Pradesh) plant which was notorious for being in an area with law-and-order problems.

> 'The scariest incident in my life was when I joined Delhi as a branch manager in 1982. Haryana was under the Delhi branch and we were not very strong there. I visited the then-largest dealer in Yamuna-Nagar and a few months later I got a call from him [Lalaji]. Lalaji told me to come to his shop at 4 p.m. the next day, dressed in good clothes [Anand usually wore an Asian Paints shirt].
>
> 'Lalaji told me that a potential suitor was coming to see his daughter for the prospect of marriage. But Lalaji wasn't very fluent in spoken English and wanted me next to him. Lalaji had met me only once and yet he had absolute faith that an Asian Paints employee would not misguide him—that too an employee who was a bachelor, or roughly the same age as the potential suitor, and had to help make a decision that would shape the lives of two people. So, we met the boy and talked for about half an hour with him. Lalaji asked me, "*Ladka kaisa laga* [how did you like the boy]?" I told him the boy was educated, he has a decent job and should have a good future and eventually, they got married. Luckily for me, the marriage lasted.'

Imagine for a moment that this same Anand at one time had bodyguards with him when he was at the Kasna plant and yet, for him, the scariest incident was when he was called upon to give his opinion over an important decision for a dealer.

Anand also told me about the Diwali practice at Asian Paints. Given the importance of the season for paint dealers, it is a practice in the industry for bosses to meet the dealers during the festival. In the case of Asian Paints, all four founders would personally go to the market and visit dealers during the festival to meet them and offer greetings. This practice continued, and as Asian Paints grew larger, the dealers would be divided among the founders and other senior employees. 'Even the smallest dealer must be visited,' Anand told me. Dealer relationships nurtured as part of corporate culture pay off rich dividends over the long term.

2. Bharat Puri—Having Chaat with Dealers

Bharat Puri, managing director of Pidilite, PGDM from IIMA, spent sixteen years at Asian Paints (1982–99) and was among the most influential employees at the company, shaping its marketing and advertising strategies in the 1980s and 1990s.

He told me,

> 'I spent three years in Uttar Pradesh (UP). As a young bachelor in my twenties, I would happily sit in dealer shops, listen to their problems and help them out. We called it kitchen relationships at Asian Paints. I'd have chaat [a street food famous in UP] with them on the streets. The second-largest dealer even invited me over to his house to be an arbiter in a family dispute!
>
> 'When the branch became computerized in the early 1980s, the dealers would line up at the branch office to see the machines. They were fascinated to see a dot matrix printer for the very first time in their lives. If the competition was focused on giving discounts to dealers, we focused on the smaller things, arbiter working with painters, helping the dealers, doing things out of the box.'

Backing up Anand's (who incidentally was Puri's successor in Bombay when he left to join Cadbury in 1998) story mentioned above, Puri said 'There are enough and plenty of stories of Asian Paints employees being called by dealers to help them choose spouses for their children.'

Puri recalled an incident from 1984 when the anti-Sikh riots had severely hit the northern states of India.

> Unfortunately, the riots were around the auspicious festival of Diwali which is the peak season for the paints industry. One of our exclusive dealers in the north had gotten very badly impacted and was asking for help. He had no stock and no money to

pay even if we sent it to him. The Mumbai office was closed for Diwali and in those times, there were no mobile phones for us to immediately call up our seniors to ask for ideas or take approvals. The poor guy told me that if he didn't open up his shop and make some sales, his business would be finished. We told him we would restock his shop and send him a bill which he could pay at the end of the year. He was most thankful.

'It turned out that the dealer knew Champakbhai and wrote him a letter, acknowledging what I'd done. Champakbhai came out of his cabin demanding to know who this Puri fellow was. The staff got scared and asked if I'd be reprimanded. Champakbhai said, "No, no. I want to meet him. He did the right thing. These are Asian Paints' values that he was upholding."'

What Did the Competition Miss?

Why did the competition miss all of this back then? Possibly because they never took Asian Paints seriously. Asian Paints initiatives through the 1950s and 1960s were a great sign of strategic intent. I take the term from the famous 1989 column in *Harvard Business Review* (HBR) by management gurus Gary Hamel and C.K. Prahalad on how Japanese companies beat their Western counterparts in the 1980s.

A 2005 HBR online article[3] summarizes Hamel and Prahalad's thesis that 'Western companies focus on trimming their ambitions to match resources and, as a result, search only for advantages they can sustain. By contrast, Japanese corporations leverage resources by accelerating the pace of organizational learning and trying to attain seemingly impossible goals. These firms foster the desire to succeed among their employees and maintain it by spreading the vision of global leadership. This is how Canon sought to "beat Xerox" and Komatsu set out to "encircle Caterpillar".'

In the original column, part of the wonderful 'HBR at 100' compilation, the authors detail further,

[3] Gary Hamel and C.K. Prahalad, 'Strategic Intent', *Harvard Business Review*, July–August 2005, https://hbr.org/2005/07/strategic-intent.

'Think back: in 1970, few Japanese companies possessed the resource base, manufacturing volume, or technical prowess of US and European industry leaders. Komatsu was less than 35 per cent as large as Caterpillar (measured by sales), was scarcely represented outside Japan, and relied on just one product line—small bulldozers—for most of its revenue. Honda was smaller than American Motors and had not yet begun to export cars to the United States. Canon's first halting steps in the reprographics business looked pitifully small compared with the $4 billion Xerox powerhouse.

'If Western managers had extended their competitor analysis to include these companies, it would merely have underlined how dramatic the resource discrepancies between them were. Yet by 1985, Komatsu was a $2.8 billion company with a product scope encompassing a broad range of earth-moving equipment, industrial robots and semiconductors. Honda manufactured almost as many cars worldwide in 1987 as Chrysler. Canon matched Xerox's global unit market share.

'The lesson is clear: assessing the current tactical advantages of known competitors will not help you understand the resolution, stamina or inventiveness of potential competitors.'

Foreign competition probably never took Asian Paints seriously and by the time they did, it was too late. In 1967, twenty-five years after it started, with sales of Rs 4.5 crore, Asian Paints nudged past Shalimar Paints as India's largest paints company—a status it holds even today. Most market leaders rest on their laurels, even become complacent and continue with the same methods that brought them to #1.

Not Asian Paints. Champakbhai, Chimanbhai and Suryakantbhai had crossed fifty years of age. Forget next year, they had their eyes decades ahead. They were hungry for growth, and nothing would stop them. If the 1950s and the 1960s were the decades of the chemist, the 1970s would herald the era of the MBAs.

1960—A Tragedy among the Founders

One of the biggest tragedies to hit Asian Paints very early on was the unexpected death of Arvindbhai in 1960. All the families, including the children, had gone on a pilgrimage together during which Arvindbhai passed away unexpectedly and at a very young age. The families stood together in complete solidarity and Veenaben replaced Arvindbhai on the board, a position she held till the 1990s when her sons Abhay and Amar Vakil joined the board.

The death also hit the company hard. Arvindbhai was responsible for many important areas in Asian Paints, including expansion across India and overseas as well. He was also responsible for arranging financing from banks for the company in its early days. His loss was impossible to fill, as the founders realized, and showed the importance of having a second line of defence that could step up in case of emergencies. That second line of defence was already being built in the late 1950s.

Going Beyond Family to Strengthen Talent

It is always difficult for families to give an outsider control of any part of their business. Family businesses run on trust, and the first people you trust are your own family, friends and people of your own community. This works in most cases. But Champakbhai and the founders knew that they possessed neither the technical qualifications to make paints nor the marketing brilliance to expand all over India. Hiring non-family professionals was, therefore, a necessity if they wanted to achieve their ambitions. They started with baby steps in the 1950s, and by 1974, they were the largest paints company hiring out of the IIMs (as we will see in Chapter 6). Here are two of the most influential people to join Asian Paints early on.

D. Madhukar—An Early Pillar

In 1958, there was one family of hires who proved valuable and whose impact would play out over the longer term. In all my interviews, I am not exactly sure where Champakbhai got the idea to hire someone with a master's degree in political science from Osmania University. One popular theory takes the origin story to one Dongargaoker Ramchander, the branch manager of the Asian Paints Hyderabad or Secunderabad branch; he was the eldest of the three Dongargaoker brothers—Ramchander, Kishan and Madhukar.

All three brothers worked for Asian Paints. Ramchander was the branch manager at Hyderabad, Kishan joined in Bengaluru, went on to become sales manager and eventually took up a paints agency in east India, and Madhukar—the youngest—scaled the greatest heights.

The story goes that Ramchander introduced Madhukar, who was then a lecturer in Hyderabad, to Champakbhai during one of Champakbhai's visits to the Hyderabad branch. Madhukar graduated from Nizam College and obtained his master's degree in political science from Osmania University in 1957. After spending a year at that university as a lecturer in political science, he joined the then Asian Oil & Paint Co. in 1958, at the age of thirty-four. Champakbhai recognized the spark in Madhukar and gave him all the room to grow, a hallmark of Champakbhai that would become part of the Asian Paints DNA.

Madhukar (as per some interviews I had) joined as an executive assistant to Champakbhai and then worked across almost all areas from the factory to marketing efforts. He was instrumental in formulating the open markets policy and in convincing Champakbhai to hire MBAs from the IIMs, a practice that would change Asian Paints after 1968.

Madhukar rose to become an executive director at Asian Paints, arguably the senior-most position that a non-family board member could hold in that era. He worked for almost thirteen years at Asian Paints (1958–71), after which he left to join British Paints where he was appointed the chief executive and subsequently the managing director in July 1973. Unfortunately, he passed away early at the age of forty-seven in 1980. The following paragraphs on him are from the Indian Paints Association 1989 book:

> Meticulous in approach, indefatigable in work, Madhukar, with a keen eye to recognize and reward merit, established himself with ease as the leader in any group.
>
> A man with zest for life, he died young on 21st July 1980, leaving behind his widow, Savita and daughter, Sita (now settled in Pune), deeply mourned by all in the industry and the association.
>
> A man who contributed immensely to the working of the Indian Paint Association, he was twice its president during the periods 1969–70 and during 1977–78.

Chari—The 'Best Boss' for Many

In college, Madhukar had a friend, K. Rajagopalachari, or just 'Chari'. While Madhukar did his master's in political science, Chari got his law degree from the Law College of Osmania University and—while working at Asian Paints—a postgraduate diploma in industrial management from the University of Bombay in 1964. Madhukar introduced Chari to Champakbhai.

Chari joined Asian Paints on 31 March 1959, staying there till his last day when he passed away on 14 March 2005—a stint of forty-six years. On page 4 of its 2005 annual report, on the page that lists the Board of Directors, Asian Paints carried a heartfelt tribute to Chari with the words 'Leader, Philosopher and Mentor' under his photo. This is an extract from Chairman Ashwin Choksi's annual letter, which shows the magnitude of Chari's contribution to Asian Paints:

> I would also like to make a special mention of Mr K. Rajagopalachari, whose demise in March this year ended a forty-six-year-long association with the Company. Well read in history and law, Mr Rajagopalachari brought to bear his immense knowledge of both to shape strategy. His sense of professionalism, fair play, equity, and personal values inspired colleagues and associates. Asian Paints will miss him.

Chari's contribution—as the obituary above reflects—would play a very important role for Asian Paints. In introducing Chari to Champakbhai in the late 1950s, Madhukar indirectly had a role to play in installing a stalwart in the company. In repeated interviews with family and ex-employees, Chari emerged as one of the most influential seniors at Asian Paints with praise ranging from best boss, best friend, to best drinking partner. Most importantly, Chari would go on to become the most enduring shock absorber between the founding families and the professionals.

Anything tricky to communicate from both sides would go via Chari. Without being a family member of either, he was an important family member of the company. Among his many quirks were long silences that he used well during interviews. Vivek Patwardhan spent more than thirty-four years (1975–2009) at Asian Paints, joining as a welfare officer and rising to vice president–HR; he is now an executive coach and HR consultant. He was also Chari's junior, and in a moving tribute,[4] he described this quirk as follows:

> He would slide slowly in his chair during a long discussion and you could see only the top of his head and his large eyes at the edge of the table. In such a position he would stare at you for minutes, introducing long pauses in conversations, making you very uncomfortable. Sometimes he would hold a

[4] Vivek Patwardhan, 'Carry the Burden on My Head', http://vivekvsp.com/i-carry-the-burden-on-my-head/, accessed on 7 January 2024.

foot ruler in hand and he would hold it on table as if he was holding a mast of a ship. Sometimes you would get a feeling of being 'measured' when he engaged in intense discussions and also when he maintained long silence.

Chari worked with three generations of founders and innumerable younger professional managers, some of whom are CEOs of leading companies today. In some interviews with employees and family, I've seen them become emotional, even moved to tears when they remembered their times with Chari.

If Champakbhai had the support of Sushilaben and Ashvinaben at home, he had the support of people like Nadkarni, Madhukar and Chari at work by the late 1950s—a few more would join in the 1960s. Success stories are built on many shoulders even if the leader takes all the credit. But without the able and strong support of these shoulders, no leader can carry the weight of his ambitions or achieve great success.

The tradition of strong leadership is integral to Asian Paints' success. In 2009, the management took a major step by appointing a non-family member as MD/CEO, trusting P.M. Murty for the job. He would be replaced by another veteran, K.B.S. Anand, and then by the current CEO, Amit Syngle.

Table 3.1: Managing directors/CEOs at Asian Paints (1978 onward)

Years	Names
1978 to 1984	Champaklal Choksey and Suryakant Dani
1984 to 1997	Ashwin Choksi and Atul Choksey
1998	Ashwin Choksi
1999 to 2008	Ashwin S. Dani and Abhay A. Vakil
2009 to 2012	P.M. Murty
2012 to 2019	K.B.S. Anand
2020 till date	Amit Syngle

(Source: Annual reports. Note: Years are financial years as per annual reports.)

When corporate governance norms changed in India to increase the number of independent directors, Asian Paints went a step further. Saurabh Mukherjea has chronicled this well in *The Unusual Billionaires* where he writes, 'Asian Paints is among that rare breed of companies whose boards are truly independent.' These directors are listed in the table below.

Table 3.2: Non-family independent directors at Asian Paints (1978 onward)

Names	Years
Bhupatrai Ghia	1978 to 1990
Harshad N. Kapadia	1978 to 1997
K. Rajagopalachari	1984 to 2005
M.G. Patel	1987 to 2005
Tarjani Vakil	1999 to 2013
Dipankar Basu	2000 to 2017
R.A. Shah	2001 to 2014
S. Sivaram	2001 to 2022
Mahendra Shah	2001 to 2019
S. Ramadorai	2010 to 2019
M.K. Sharma	2013 to 2022
Deepak M. Satwalekar	2000 till date
Vibha Paul Rishi	2014 till date
R. Seshasayee	2017 till date
Suresh Narayanan	2019 till date
Pallavi Shroff	2019 till date
Milind Sarwate	2022 till date

(Source: Annual reports. Note: Years are financial years as per annual reports.)

Chapter 4

The Rise of the Chemist

'Chemistry is change and change is the core of your belief system. Which is good because that's what we need more of—people who refuse to accept the status quo, who aren't afraid to take on the unacceptable.'

—Bonnie Garmus, *Lessons in Chemistry*

India went through a tough time in its third decade of freedom from British Rule. India fought two significant wars with its neighbours—against China in 1962 and Pakistan in 1965. Within India as well there were insurgencies in North-east (1964) and Naxalites/Maoists in 1967. It lost two prime ministers within two years—Pandit Jawaharlal Nehru in 1964 and Lal Bahadur Shastri in 1967. India had a drought in 1965 and 1966 and was dependent on the USA for food. Bihar had a famine in 1966/67. Towards the end of the decade, the Indira Gandhi-led Congress government had nationalized fourteen banks. Despite this tough macroeconomic backdrop, Asian Paints continued to expand and increase capacity, eyeing new frontiers.

In 1958, Asian Paints opened its first major production facility in Bhandup. The Bhandup factory, which was instrumental in transforming the company in the 1960s and taking it to the #1 spot in 1968, was finally shut down in 2014, after serving the company faithfully for fifty-six years.

Located on the twenty-one-km-long snaking Dr Lal Bahadur Shastri Marg (or simply LBS in Mumbai parlance) that connects Sion in Central Mumbai to Thane in Northern Mumbai, the Asian Paints factory was one such landmark that seasoned Mumbaikars will remember even today, even as factories from that era are slowly shutting down to be replaced with high-rise residential complexes and malls.

While Asian Paints became the largest paints company in India in 1967, the decade building up to this achievement was arguably the most central to its identity. This was the time when the founding partners truly began the process of building an institution that outlived all of them when they could have been very content with remaining a small-scale unit operating out of a small factory in Matunga. In this chapter, we look at three reasons why this decade was important and how Asian Paints strengthened its bench of professional talent during this period.

There are three major reasons why 1957 to 1967 was so important for Asian Paints.

Reason 1: From Matunga to Bhandup

The Matunga factory lease was signed in 1947, and by the early 1950s, it was overflowing with stocks of raw materials and finished goods, both of which are stored in large containers that occupy a lot of space. With crude oil and its derivates involved in the manufacturing process, there was hazardous material lying around all the time. The shift from garages and small factories in Bhuleshwar to Matunga was one thing but the decision to move to a far-flung suburb was a leap of faith.

Asian Paints bought a large parcel of land (more than eight acres) in an area that was getting included within Mumbai city limits. Bhandup transformed Asian Paints, giving the four partners the space and freedom to plan their future. If the partners moved facilities twice since inception (from the original garage to the second small factory and from there to

Matunga), then Bhandup saw them through for the next twenty years (the Ankleshwar plant was commissioned in 1981) and served the company for more than twenty years. The famous computer that Asian Paints would purchase in the early 1970s was installed at Bhandup, as we will see later in this book. The R&D lab that became a cornerstone of Asian Paints' success in its early years was also at Bhandup.

The move was far-sighted and the first of many such decisions made by Asian Paints. If the founders wanted, they could have been complacent and stayed within their comfort zone (either in products or in geographical areas or both), as many family-run businesses prefer doing after they have an established product.

But buying a large plot of land in a new and upcoming part of Bombay shows the confidence they had in their product and how much they were willing to bet on it. At the age of twenty, Champakbhai left his family, accepted Suryakantbhai's offer and started Neptune Trading Agency. By the age of forty-two, Champakbhai was well ensconced within the Indian paints industry and Asian Paints had started their first large paints manufacturing facility. Hindsight tells us that this was just the beginning.

Reason 2: Right Place, Right Time

With the Industrial Policy Resolution 1948, India was taking firm steps to usher in the industrial era.[1] In the 1950s, Indian manufacturing—both private sector and public sector—was taking major steps in investment. So, while on the one hand, giant public sector undertakings (PSUs) like Hindustan Steel Limited (eventually, SAIL) and Hindustan Machine Tools (HMT) were being formed, some of India's best-known consumer brands—the Ambassador car, Godrej typewriter, Bajaj Scooter and Usha sewing machines—were being launched. For the first time in India, liquified petroleum gas (LPG) under the trade name 'Burshane'

[1] Professor Tirthankar Roy, *A Business History of India*, Chapter 7, Cambridge University Press, 2018.

was launched[2] in Mumbai by Burmah Shell as a move towards cleaner cooking fuels began, away from kerosene-filled stoves.

From a largely unorganized sector with small-scale industries, India was slowly moving towards a more formal structure, a transition that continues even today. The share of the organized sector in net domestic product increased[3] to 20 per cent in 1960–61 from 15 per cent in 1950–51. The paints industry grew in tandem.

By 1961, the capacity of the paints industry rose to 84,900 tons from 64,800 tons in 1951—but the number of units had increased only by three, to fifty-three from fifty during the same period, which showed that existing paint companies had ramped up investment. The paints industry was also characterized by unorganized, smaller-scale industries that impacted overall demand with cheaper and inferior-quality paints. As mentioned in the previous chapters, larger paints players were uniting under industry organizations (the merger of IPMA and the Paints Federation in 1960 to form the Indian Paints Association) to lobby with the government.

The results were efforts such as a move towards quality standards by the government so that at least a bare minimum quality was established and certified; and the sale of paints by volume instead of weight. Selling by weight resulted[4] in price cutting because some manufacturers would load paints with chemicals called extenders which would increase the weight but lower the quality. Champakbhai was already part of the paints associations and could see that the paints industry was consolidating in the 1950s and 1960s. Hence, commencing the Bhandup factory in 1958 would place Asian Paints in the right place at the right time.

---

[2] Bharat Petroleum, 'About BPCL', https://www.bharatpetroleum.in/About-BPCL/Our-Journey/A-pioneering-approach.aspx, accessed on 7 January 2024.

[3] EPW, 'Technological Change in the Indian Economy, https://www.jstor.org/stable/4356840, accessed on 7 January 2024.

[4] *Indian Paints Association* (1989), p. 165.

Reason 3: The Rise of the Chemist

It was one thing for the founders in their early days to crush pigment and resin and sell paint in cans door to door on cycles. But this was the era when paints were imported, and paints technology was the preserve of foreigners. So, how did the founders get the technical abilities to make decorative paints for consumers? They went straight to the source of the best talent. At that time, this was the University Department of Chemical Technology (UDCT, now known as the Institute of Chemical Technology), a department of Bombay University (as it was known then).

Formed in 1933 and located in Matunga, UDCT had fast become one of India's premier engineering colleges. This is how one of many famous alumni of UDCT, Narotam Seksharia (founder of Gujarat Ambuja Cement) described his times there in his memoir,[5] 'My four years at UDCT were extremely productive and I benefited from them tremendously. Four rigorous years in a chemical engineering college prepare you for more than running a chemical plant. They help you learn to think logically and laterally, understand intricate processes and solve complex problems.'

Jairam Nadkarni (JMN)—The Chemist Who Changed Asian Paints

The most influential hire from UDCT for Asian Paints would be one of its gold medallists, Jairam Mangesh Nadkarni. Champakbhai was quoted[6] as saying, 'The moment Nadkarni took over, everything changed for Asian Paints.' Atul Choksey told me,

> 'From my father to the paints industry, everyone regarded Nadkarni as the best polymer scientist at that time. As far as paints technology and polymerization are concerned, he was

---

[5] Narotam Seksharia, *The Ambuja Story*, HarperBusiness 2021.

[6] Interview with A. Raghavan for *Paint India Magazine* (also ref. next footnote).

a genius. There was nobody like him because he developed products that were better than foreign competition who had the technical support of their parent company abroad. Nadkarni played a very important role at Asian Paints and without him, there would have been a vacuum in technology.'

In 1952, Nadkarni[7] returned to India from Germany after dropping out of a scholarship-funded PhD at the Technische Universität Berlin, which he left to take care of his father. Nadkarni's friend introduced him to the founders of Asian Paints. The rest was history. Nadkarni joined as chief chemist, established Asian Paints' first paint R&D laboratory in 1953, and became Asian Paints' first technical director. He was instrumental in the design and structure of the Bhandup factory and responsible for transforming and upgrading the Asian Paints product line to synthetic enamels (Apcolite), oil-bound distemper (Tractor), and a variety of other finishes and varnishes—and all of this at a lower cost than foreign competitors.

He was the pioneer of rosinated alkyd resins (that hasten drying and improve hardness), making them at the R&D lab. This was a significant breakthrough since raw materials are a major chunk of costs in the manufacture of paints. Nadkarni was imaginative with ideas such as repurposing used machinery given the tight budget in those days. Nadkarni was with Asian Paints for eight years. In 1960, he started a new endeavour with his college friend, J.M. 'Mota' Chudasama, with the company Bombay Paints—more details on Nadkarni and his family are available on the Nadkarni Specialty Polymers and Coating website mentioned in the footnotes.

From Moneylenders to Banks

Nadkarni's efforts in the technical department gave the founders breathing space to focus on raising funds for expansion. Working

[7] Nadkarni, 'About Us', https://www.nadkarnispc.com/about-us/

capital is the most critical area for the paints business and an area where Asian Paints would go on to make significant progress. But in its early days, when Asian Paints was too small to qualify for a bank loan, the founders would control working capital by reducing customers who demanded too long a period to pay their dues, keeping tight control on inventories and cutting costs.

The founders were also dependent on moneylenders for funds; for example, Jamnadas Vora and his son who are mentioned in earlier chapters. Funds borrowed from unorganized and unofficial sources in India are always expensive, with interest rates of more than 2–3 per cent per month even today. Getting bank loans at that time was also a function of knowing the staff who worked at the bank.

Asian Paints was finally able to get a small overdraft facility from a bank in 1956. With sales growth continuing, the bank followed the overdraft with a term loan and once Asian Paints had established a track record, they went on to get a cash-credit facility from a large bank. Thus, slowly and surely Asian Paints made the transition from informal sources of funds to the formal system of banking, reducing their cost of loans and helping them plan their next phase of expansion.

First Experience of Replacing Talent

When Nadkarni left in 1960, Champakbhai and the founders got their first taste of the void created when high-quality talent leaves the company, especially in a complex technical area. Getting talent from competition was not an option since no one from a foreign company would join an Indian competitor of little repute. Raising talent within would not have been possible then since the laboratory was small and so was Nadkarni's team.

Paint technicians and chemists were highly specialized roles for which talent was in short supply in an industry still dominated by large foreign companies and proliferated by smaller unorganized players. The IPA newly formed in 1960 had also tried and largely given up efforts to set up cooperative research laboratories among members. After all, if a company invests heavily in talent and facilities, why would it share this with the competition?

As mentioned in the previous chapter, in the mid-1950s, Champakbhai had also begun his journey in the paints industry where he would eventually become a leader in an almost statesman like role. Among the four founders, Champakbhai was the designated one to represent Asian Paints in industry bodies like IPMA and the Paints Federation.

He progressed so well that by the late-1950s he was Chairman of the Western Zone of the IPMA. Champakbhai was among the speakers at the very first All India Paint Conference held at Kanpur in 1959 and was instrumental in getting the next year's conference to be held in Bombay.

Thus, Champakbhai had spent enough time with the Paints Federation and the IPMA to know all the large players in the paints industry and how the industry worked. Champakbhai thought of technical collaborations with foreign giants like Kansai Paints and Nippon Paints and even travelled to Japan.

But in the end, Champakbhai knew that his strategy of pursuing local talent was the right one. UDCT's alumni were a closely connected group of people and word usually gets around when there are job vacancies. In 1961, Champakbhai hired two UDCT engineers—Kamalaksha Ganapati Kudva and Chidanand Jayram Bhumkar. Between the two, K.G. Kudva was senior and joined as technical director, the post vacated by Nadkarni.

Kudva and Bhumkar—Leading the Technical Department

Kudva's choice was interesting because of his rich educational background and work experience. He was older than Nadkarni and highly educated and decorated. He had done his bachelor's (BSc Tech), master's (MSc Tech) and PhD from UDCT. In 1944, he went to Brooklyn Technical, New York (which became

NYU Tandon School of Engineering), studying chemistry of high polymers, under the famous Professor Herman Francis Mark.[8] Thereafter, he proceeded to the University of Louisville, Kentucky, on a fellowship at the Institute of Industrial Research and even worked at Reliance Varnish Company, Louisville, now part of AkzoNobel.

Kudva knew the iconoclast educator,[9] Professor N.R. Kamath, who had a major influence on the formative years of IIT Bombay and the chemical engineering profession in India. Kamath and Kudva were among the founders[10] of the Colour Society which was formed to further scientific and technology development in the paints industry. Both also spoke at the paint conferences organized by the IPA.

In his previous role at Hardcastle and Waud Manufacturing Company, Kudva had[11] developed surface-coating resins, synthetic resins-based acid and chemical-resisting cement, insulating varnishes and compounds, and a host of other products. He had written many original publications and held fourteen patents based mostly on the uses of Cashewnut Shell Liquid.

I spoke to Pramila Kudva, daughter-in-law of Kudva, who told me, 'Dr Kudva was the first PhD from UDCT. Professor Kamath and Dr Kudva were contemporaries in that era. Dr Kudva worked at Asian Paints for six years from 1961 to 1967 at the Bhandup factory and specialized in the research function.'

The story around hiring C.J. Bhumkar is interesting. I met Mrs Asha Bhumkar, his wife, who recalled Bhumkar's interview

---

[8] Wikipedia contributors, Herman Francis Mark, https://en.wikipedia.org/wiki/Herman_Francis_Mark, accessed on 7 January 2024.

[9] Queenbee, 'N.R. Kamath: An Iconoclast and an Educator', Fundamatics https://fundamatics.net/article/n-r-kamath-an-iconoclast-and-an-educator/, accessed on 7 January 2024.

[10] Colour Society, 'About Us', https://coloursociety.com/about-us/, accessed on 7 January 2024.

[11] Obituary of Dr Kudva in *Paints India Magazine*, August 1991.

and told me, 'There was a technical point of difference where Mr Bhumkar was right and the person who took the interview was wrong. But Mr Bhumkar stood his ground and came home wondering if he would get the job. Champakbhai came to know that Mr Bhumkar was right, and he got the job.'

Early Innovations in Products

In 1961, a young twenty-three-year-old student from Kanpur studying at Harcourt Butler Technical Institute (HBTI, now known as HBT University) visited the Bhandup factory, as part of industry visits and study tours organized by his college. As he toured the factory, he thought this was the paints company he would like to work for. That student was Pramesh Narian Khanna, who joined Asian Paints in 1962 and worked there for the next forty-two years, of which the first sixteen years were spent at the Bhandup factory and the next twenty-six in overseas ventures.

In a moving memoir written for Asian Paints, Khanna wrote about his times at Asian Paints. After completing his master's degree (MSc-tech) in paints technology from HBTI, Kanpur, he was called for an interview at Asian Paints, Bombay and offered the job of senior chemist under Kudva. When he was comfortable in R&D (where he had worked for eight years), he was asked to move to production. He overcame his initial reluctance after being persuaded by both Madhukar and Chari and recalled a piece of advice he got from Madhukar early in his career, 'If you want to come up in life, you must not specialize in one field, but should have a wide range of experiences.'

During 1962–70, he wrote about how the most popular product then was Apcolite Synthetic Enamel, and water-based paints were slowly gaining popularity, an area where Asian Paints had only one product—the Tractor Oil Bound Distemper. Given the need to expand their range, a lot of laboratory work was done, and the following products were developed:

Table 4.1: Products developed at Asian Paints during the 1960s and 1970s

#	Product description
1	Acrylic distemper
2	100 per cent acrylic paint for exterior use
3	A middling-quality water base paint called DECOPLAST for exterior and interior use
4	Apcolite Universal Stainers—which could be used to tint the white water-based as well as oil-based paints by the painters at the site
5	Majiktouch—this was a unique concept, wherein necessary tinters were premixed and packed in a collapsible tube. One tube was needed for four-litres of white base paint to give the desired colour
6	Chemical-resistant paints (CRPs) such as epoxies, chloro-rubber, vinyl, etc.
7	Apcodur 695—a special product for urea prill towers
8	CRPs—chemical-resistant paints like epoxies, chloro-rubber, vinyl, etc.
9	Apcodur 695—special product for urea prill towers

(Source: P.N. Khanna memoirs written for Asian Paints)

In just under two decades (1942 to 1958), Asian Paints went from a small, local paints manufacturing unit operating from garages to a full-blown factory with R&D labs run by highly trained and qualified professionals. The next generation of chemists and engineers—in the form of Khanna and Bhumkar—were also being trained to ensure that the company maintained and grew its competitive advantages.

Champakbhai and the founders were confident that decorative paints, which was still smaller than the industrial segment, was where Asian Paints could build its competitive advantage even if it meant taking on foreign competition. While the decorative market was new, there was space to establish a product that consumers would remember and could hence have potentially higher margins than the price-led industrial segment. Having the product is one thing but selling it in an industry dominated by foreign giants was another challenge, as we will see in the next chapter.

Strengthening the Bench

After Madhukar and Chari another key hire, from what I gathered from my conversation with ex-employees, was C.V. Abraham who joined on 1 December 1960. Between themselves, Abraham, Madhukar and Chari would be the first ones to take interviews at the IIMs in the coming decades. It was to Madhukar and Chari's credit and capability that they excelled at Asian Paints, irrespective of their educational background; Madhukar was a professor in political science and Chari was a lawyer. Abraham continued this tradition. He was a chartered accountant who would go on to become the sales manager in 1972 and the marketing manager in 1978.

One story about Abraham was that he was working in Bengaluru and started studying for the CA exams with the plan of starting his own business. Champakbhai spotted him and brought him to Mumbai. Abraham retired from Asian Paints in 1992, spending thirty-two years at the company and passed away in 2012 at the age of eighty. He was fondly remembered in many of my conversations with ex-employees.

After Abraham, the next two key hires would prove to be Bipin Jhaveri and B.R. Trivedi. Jhaveri was Champakbhai's nephew and joined Asian Paints in 1962. In those days, Asian Paints was a private limited company, and the concepts of corporate governance were not as prevalent as they are today. Irrespective of his relationship with Champakbhai, Jhaveri was also highly educated with both a chartered accountant degree and a company secretary degree, besides being a double graduate in arts and commerce. Jhaveri established his merit over the years as a CFO who navigated Asian Paints through important phases such as its expansions in Ankleshwar, Patancheru and Kasna as well as the IPO in 1982. Jhaveri left Asian Paints, along with Champakbhai, in 1997, having stayed with the company for thirty-five years.

Bhanushankar (B.R.) Trivedi came via a priest (or a Pandit-ji) that the Choksey family knew, and even though he wasn't as educationally qualified as the others, that never stopped him from proving his worth and becoming essential to Asian Paints. Trivedi joined in 1965 and worked in multiple roles at Asian Paints, from handling the Ahmedabad branch to becoming the exports manager.

He earned the trust of the founders, especially Champakbhai, and the employees over time. 'Once an argument broke out at the Bhandup factory between a few senior employees which escalated to the extent that all three threatened to resign. Champakbhai told Trivedi to rush to Bhandup and by the end of the day, all three employees went home happy,' Atul Choksey told me, recalling Trivedi.

These five hires—Madhukar (1958), Chari (1959), Abraham (1960), Jhaveri (1962) and Trivedi (1965)—were instrumental in creating a strong and enduring management layer before the MBAs were hired and before the second generation of founders had joined the company. All five of them were diverse, educated in differing fields (except Trivedi), and switched between many roles from the factory to marketing to exports to hiring.

Thus, the five hires were instrumental in placing Asian Paints at the number one spot by 1967 and, more importantly, creating an atmosphere of professionalism in a family-run business. It was as if Champakbhai had a knack for spotting talent in the unlikeliest of places and pointing them in a direction where they would excel at Asian Paints.

If there is one sombre and yet respectful sign of longevity at an organization, it is when the organization's name is carried next to the employee's name in his obituary. This was a tradition with older generations, where staying for long periods in one job was considered normal and even desirable, given the stability it offered to the employee and their family. Perhaps this was also a function of fewer job opportunities in that era. But when a family carries the company's name (for example,[12] 'ex-Asian Paints' in the case of C.V. Abraham) in the obituary of their loved one, then surely that is a sign of how significant that company was in their lives.

There were many employees for whom Asian Paints was the only job they had, the first job they signed up for and the company they retired from, spending anywhere between twenty-five to forty years, with K.B.S. Anand being the most recent and prominent one. Anand stepped down in 2019 after spending forty years in the company. Many of these employees—now in their seventies and eighties—are in touch with each other even today and fondly recall their times at Asian Paints.

[12] ToI Staff, 'C V Abraham', *Times of India*, 15 October 2016, https://timesofindia.indiatimes.com/c-v-abraham/articleshow/54868726.cms.

Chapter 5

Geetanjali

Har ghar chup chap se ye kehta hai
ke andar isme kaun rehta hai
chhat batati hai ye kiska aasman hai
rang kehte hain kiska ye jahan hai
kamron main kiski kalpana jhalakti hai
is farsh par nange pair kiske bachhe chalte hai
kaun chun chun ke isse pyar se sajata hai
kaun is makan main apna ghar basata hai
har ghar chup chap se ye kehta hai
ke undar isme kaun rehta hai

Loosely translated, this means:

Each house silently has something to say, about the people who stay within; the roof tells you whose sky it is, the colours tell you whose world it is; the rooms give a glimpse of ideas, the floors ring with the bare feet of children, who decorates each part with love; who makes a home within the house, each house has something to say, about the people who stay within.

In the early 2000s Piyush Pandey, chairman and creative director of Ogilvy & Mather wrote these moving lines on his pad at one shot, read it to himself and cried.[1] The lines were part of an ad that went on to become yet another iconic campaign

[1] Piyush Pandey, Pandemonium, 2015. Watch the ad here: https://youtu.be/983_r8uAFQI

for Asian Paints. While the ad was launched many years after Champakbhai had passed away and the Chokseys had exited Asian Paints, the sensitive, evocative and beautiful lines hit upon a deep truth—homes say a lot about the people who live within. And Geetanjali, the building the Chokseys moved into in the 1960s and continue to live in together, has its own story.

Champakbhai and his partners were busy building the foundations of Asian Paints in the late 1950s. As the company grew, so did the aspirations of the founders. When Champakbhai turned forty in 1956, he was living in a tiny flat at the Sonawala Building which was already cramped with a total of seven family members (four children, Champakbhai, Ashvinaben and Sushilaben, or Sushila-Ba, as she was affectionately addressed by all).

Like any father and any businessman, he aspired to a bigger home in an affluent area. Champakbhai was also now a leader in the paints industry (western zone) and part of many business circles as well. He had seen how the rich lived in areas like Peddar Road, Breach Candy, Malabar Hill, etc. While he was living near Mumbai Central Railway Station, like any Mumbaikar, he aspired to be closer to the sea.

The dreams came closer to reality when a group of businessmen, including Champakbhai and a few of his acquaintances (including from Asian Paints), acquired a bungalow at Gamadia Road (off Peddar Road) in the late 1950s. The bungalow belonged to a renowned doctor and the idea was for the buyers to construct a building on a commercial basis with flats/homes to be sold to a closed set of people, including themselves. Cumballa Hill is an upscale area in South Mumbai. It was less than 5 km from the Sonawala Building but a big jump in terms of ambition.

While Sonawala Building is close to Mumbai Central Terminus, Cumballa Hill is close to the sea and surrounded by areas like Altamount Road, Breach Candy and Mahalaxmi—the preserve of some of Mumbai's richest. The group of businessmen hired architects to design and contractors to construct the building, and Champakbhai would visit the site for three hours every Sunday. The building took around five to six years to build and the Chokseys moved in the early 1960s.

The nine-floor building is called Geetanjali and is located off a by-lane that connects Peddar Road and Warden Road. When he first moved in, Champakbhai bought the fourth floor where the seven family members shifted. Geetanjali would become as close to the Chokseys' hearts as did Asian Paints. A few years after they shifted, there were three major family events for the Choksey family, all of which happened at Geetanjali. In the 1960s, shortly after they shifted, there were two family weddings (Rita married Ashok Parekh and Girish married Sunita Parikh) and the arrival of Champakbhai's first grandchild, Ankur.

Large Families Need Large Spaces

Champakbhai was a busy man and yet, family remained closest to his heart. I spoke with Priti Choksey, Amit Choksey's wife, at Geetanjali. She said,

> 'Papa [Champakbhai] could see ten to twenty years ahead. When they shifted to Geetanjali, they were seven of them in one house. But Papa knew that his children would get married, and his three sons would need their own homes and space. So as the years went by, he bought homes on other floors even though no one lived in them at first—something we did not understand then. But as each son got married, they shifted to their own homes, giving them more space and independence.'

The idea embodied Champakbhai's values of a family living together (in one building) while still having their own space (separate homes). The families and their support system were, hence, in one place. When Girish shifted to his own house within Geetanjali, Champakbhai insisted that Sunita should have her own kitchen even though she would lovingly remain an integral part of the fourth floor.

Parul said, 'At that time, Papa told us that the day we felt like we always needed to be together, was when we should let people go. That is how people stay together. He believed that one should never be attached to things, thoughts, beliefs and belongings.' Kitchens worked in unison and dinner was served at 8 p.m. with attendance being compulsory for all family members. There was only one rule—no business would be discussed at the table.

Family Values Continue in the Third Generation

The tradition of family dinners continued in the third generation as well. Ankur Choksey, Girish's firstborn son, told me, 'The family had to get together in front of Dadaji. If we [the grandchildren] skipped a few times, we'd get an emotional reminder from him.' Ankur told me that Champakbhai was very hands-on with him and his younger brother Prashant. Both Ankur and Prashant did their graduation in US colleges with the blessings and guidance of Champakbhai. 'Those days, we didn't have a mobile so we'd call home once every week or ten days and talk with Dadaji,' Ankur told me. Later when Ankur spent some time learning the ropes at Asian Paints, Champakbhai would be keenly interested in what Ankur was learning right down to details. As he did for his sons, Champakbhai was also clear that his grandchildren would not join Asian Paints and would either join their father's business or start their own. 'This wasn't a choice whether we liked it or not. If Dadaji says it [be in our own business] has to be done, then it has to be done. We took it as a challenge to chart our own course in life and as we realized later, he was right,' Ankur told me.

Champakbhai was a doting grandfather and watching his grandchildren grow before him was a great experience of his life. Both Ankur and Prashant spent time at Asian Paints before moving on to their respective companies. Ankur followed in his father's footsteps and took charge at Choksey Chemicals. Prashant runs Colortek India, a manufacturer of liquid colourants and additives for plastic and polyurethane industries. Prashant is also an investor and among the founders of Mumbai Angels, a funding platform for start-ups.

As we can see in the family tree on page xvi, Champakbhai's grandchildren also include Devaki Trivedi and Janaki Trivedi (Rita's daughters), Abhiraj Choksey and Devanshi Jalan (Atul Choksey's son and daughter respectively), and Namrata Doshi and Ankita Khatau (Amit's daughters).

Closely Knit Families in the First Generation

Initially, three of four families—the Chokseys, the Danis (who moved out later) and the Vakils lived at Geetanjali with the Choksis staying nearby in the vicinity. Irrespective of where they lived in that era, all four families were very close and on the best of terms. Champakbhai and Suryakantbhai would even go to the office (or Bhandup factory) together from Geetanjali in the same car to save fuel. All four families would celebrate major festivals together. The next generation would grow very close as well, travelling together for holidays.

Girish told me,

> 'My father used to take all our families together for short trips to nearby hill stations like Karjat, Lonavala, Matheran and Mahabaleshwar. He would rent a bungalow so all of us could stay together. Wherever there was a waterfall, he would take all of us and would jump straight in since he was a very good swimmer. He played games like cricket, and even cards, with all of us when we [the second generation of all families] were children. He would keep all the children together. As we grew, he would encourage us to take vacations on our own and explore areas we hadn't been to, such as Darjeeling, Sikkim, etc. In fact the first flight that all of us went together on was from Calcutta to Bagdogra, on a trip to the North-east.'

This closeness would remain for decades and the family saw many ups and downs together, including weddings and the birth of grandchildren.

Champakbhai also saw Asian Paints employees and dealers as part of his family. Hence, whenever he took his family and children on a vacation, he would ensure that they also met the dealers. Girish recalled an incident from 1964 or 1965 when the family travelled to Kanyakumari by road. In cities that had an Asian Paints branch, the branch would organize functions for the family to meet with local dealers and agents. In one such function, possibly in Coimbatore, dealers saw Amit (who had unruly hair as a child) and mistook him for Gattu, Asian Paints' famous mascot (discussed in Chapter 11). 'They even asked my father if he had gotten along Gattu during his visit. My father played along with them and told them that Amit was indeed Gattu,' Girish told me with a laugh.

One of the people influenced by Champakbhai's idea of Geetanjali is K.M. 'Kanubhai' Sheth, chairman of Great Eastern Shipping, India's largest private-sector shipping service provider. Sheth lives in the Manek tower of the twin residential building complex Jivan Manek in Malabar Hill, just 3 km south of Geetanjali. He is a family friend of the Chokseys and his wife, Jyotsna-ben was friends with Ashvinaben.

'Champakbhai and Ashvinaben would come for morning walks at Worli Sea Face, where we would join them sometimes. I adopted Champakbhai's idea of a family living within one building,' Sheth told me, adding, 'Champakbhai was a very honest, hard-working and transparent man. He had a great understanding of the business and never liked to fight. When we went for our walks, I always found him to be a very sober, calm and collected person.' Just as the Choksey family live together on separate floors in one building at Geetanjali, the Sheth family (including their next generations) live on separate floors at Manek.

Employees—An Extension of Family

If Geetanjali was home to the Chokseys, Asian Paints was like a home for many employees. Champakbhai always saw the employees at Asian Paints as his family and would help them whenever he could. A great example was C.J. Bhumkar and his family, where the friendship between the Chokseys and Bhumkars is now in its third generation. For many years, the Bhumkars would visit the Chokseys at Geetanjali on every Gudi Padva, which is considered the beginning of a new year in Maharashtra.

Bhumkar joined Asian Paints as a junior chemist under Kudva and left in 1981 as technical director—the most senior position in R&D. 'Champakbhai was a people's connector. He was all about gathering people for a common cause and for doing good work together,' Priya Bhumkar, Bhumkar's daughter-in-law told me. Champakbhai and Bhumkar's relationship was close and when Bhumkar wanted to leave Asian Paints to start his own company, Champakbhai helped him set up the business, which would eventually grow to become Soujanya Color Private Limited.

In October 1986, a decade after he left Asian Paints, Bhumkar suffered from a heart attack where he needed to undergo angioplasty and a bypass surgery. He had to stay in Jaslok Hospital for over a month for his treatment. 'Twice a day, home-cooked meals would come for us from Geetanjali,' said Asha Bhumkar. Priya Bhumkar added,

> 'The Chokseys were incredibly supportive during that tough time. We [Priya and her husband, Dr Ashesh Bhumkar] were young and just newly married at that time. When the doctors at Jaslok Hospital recommended a bypass, my father-in-law was reluctant. It was Champakbhai who then convinced him and gave him the confidence to undergo the surgery. The Choksey family helped us through the entire process of treatment, by not only arranging for the bypass surgery to be done in London but also connecting us to their family in London, who was of great help to us. None of this would have taken place without the help and intervention of the Chokseys.'

Work Culture as Competitive Advantage

Bosses helping employees isn't new. The idea of organizations, or CEOs, going the extra mile to help employees in their time of need was never unique to Asian Paints or the era when it grew. If kindness and compassion are universal qualities, then how does helping employees make a company great? The answer is, in building a work culture that becomes a competitive advantage.

Studying corporate performance (success and failure) has been part of business literature for decades now. The drivers of corporate greatness also seem to change as does the way to measure greatness. For example, great leadership in the form of a godlike CEO used to be a reliable mantra till it gave way to the concept of a consensus-building CEO who encourages teamwork and collaboration. Shareholder wealth was a great measure till stakeholder wealth came along. Apple is a great example of how leadership has evolved from Steve Jobs to Tim Cook, both with wildly differing styles and philosophies, and—more importantly—at differing times in Apple's life cycle.

But whatever benchmark of success you use now, corporate culture will emerge as one of many drivers. Having a great work culture alone might be neither sufficient nor necessary for a company to ensure enduring success, but a great work culture usually goes well with other drivers of success. Attracting great talent is one thing but retaining it for long periods—as Asian Paints has done in the case of many employees, including all three professional CEOs (P.M. Murty, K.B.S. Anand and the current CEO, Amit Syngle)—points to a unique culture at work. Taking care of employees is only one aspect.

John Kotter and James Heskett, professors at Harvard Business School, wrote a book titled *Corporate Culture and Performance* in 1992 establishing a link[2] between corporate culture and the economic performance of a company. The authors completed an extensive research project detailing the corporate cultures of 200 companies and how each company's culture affected its long-term performance.

---

[2] John Kotter, 'Does Corporate Culture Drive Financial Performance?', *Forbes*, 10 February 2011, https://www.forbes.com/sites/johnkotter/2011/02/10/does-corporate-culture-drive-financial-performance/?sh=4f4d78867e9e

The gap between companies with cultures that enhanced performance versus those that did not was staggering. For example, the average increase in stock price growth for the first group was 901 per cent versus 74 per cent for the second group. Kotter wrote, 'To consider that the difference between a 900 per cent and a 75 per cent appreciation in equity value is somewhat attributable to the strength of a company's corporate culture highlights the significance of this often-overlooked issue.'

Almost twenty years later in 2011, and as a follow-up to the original work, James Heskett wrote a book, *The Culture Cycle: How to Shape the Unseen Force that Transforms Performance*. Heskett makes an important point that a strong culture can contribute to an organization's success or failure. A great product, service or other significant competitive advantage can carry the performance of an organization that has a weak or counterproductive culture for only so long. There is no one ideal culture. Rather, its contribution to an organization's long-term success is determined by the extent to which it does the following:

- Sets forth values and encourages behaviours to which people at all levels in the organization can subscribe
- Attracts people who can carry out the strategy chosen for it
- Reflects the beliefs of a leadership team that occasionally revisits and reconfirms the organization's culture
- Promotes behaviours that meet the demands of the organization's competitive environment

Heskett goes on to state that cultures are formed at the earliest stages of an organization's life. Whether or not they are defined early on, cultures often reflect the values and behaviours of an organization's founder long after the founder has departed the organization.

In the case of Asian Paints, the values and vision of all founders were critical to forming the organizational culture and transitioning from a) the initial stages as a small factory that hired local labour to b) hiring chemists, and c) in the next stage, hiring professional management. None of this was simple or easy.

Freedom and Trust in Talent

Family-owned businesses have challenges attracting talent since owners/founders always occupy the top posts. So even if a professional has ambitions of rising to higher levels, they are aware that there is a logical ceiling beyond which they cannot go. This was among the reasons why Asian Paints lost first Madhukar and then Biji Kurien to British Paints in 1972. Creating this work culture in the early days of the 1960s and 1970s was a long-drawn process, even though Asian Paints was a market leader when it started hiring from IIMs. There were unexpected challenges like IIM-hires leaving the company for better prospects, uncertainty during succession planning, etc. but the founders and, more importantly, people like Chari, kept the professionals together consistently through the years creating a genuinely unique work culture.

What was the secret to Asian Paints' success? Trusting their employees to build an institution, giving them total freedom (and responsibility), and backing them to the fullest extent. 'I was just twenty-one years old when I joined Asian Paints and at that age, I was handling a sales force of people, some of whom were ten years older than me. What a learning! You just have a complete free hand—that was the great thing about Asian Paints. You own the area,' Bharat Puri told me.

I heard many such examples from ex-employees, and one incident that remained with me came from P.M. Murty. He told me how one of Asian Paints' biggest dealers had delayed payment and hence would miss out on the regular payment performance discount (RPPD) discussed later in the book. Murty went to meet him to convey this news. Obviously, the dealer was very angry that he was not getting the discount. After many cups of tea, he calmed down and told Murty a story. He said, 'This happened before and at that time, the branch manager had come to give me the same news. I protested and went to the regional sales manager who refused to send material to me until I paid up. So, I went straight to CHC [as Champakbhai was known] who I knew well.' Murty asked him what happened when we met CHC, so the dealer recalled his conversation as follows:

Dealer: 'Your fellows have stopped sending materials to me! I have some bills to pay but for some reason, I'm unable to make the payment right now, so I have come to complain to you!'

CHC: 'Whatever my fellows are, they are not mad. They are absolutely correct.'

Dealer: 'But I have come to you to appeal!'

CHC: 'Don't come to me to appeal because if I go tell them to give you even Rs 100 worth of material, you know what they will do?'

Dealer: 'No, I don't know, but surely, they will not go against you.'

CHC: 'No. You don't know my managers. They will be disappointed with me. They will tell me, "Mr chairman, what kind of a fellow are you? You keep giving us all these wonderful lectures [presumably on collections] but when one single dealer comes to you, you are succumbing." And whatever I might say, I am not willing to be seen as a hypocrite by my managers. But you are my friend and because I have known you for many years, I will give you a personal cheque, nobody will know about it. This is my personal money; I can do whatever I want. Tell me how much you want? Rs 2 lakh, Rs 3 lakh? How much? I will write the cheque here. I will tell my secretary right now.'

Dealer: 'No, it is sure, I will not take your cheque. I will manage.'

CHC: 'Are you sure? If you want help from me at a personal level, you are always welcome in my office. But if you expect me to break my own rule, the answer is a definite no.'

Murty continued his story with the dealer, 'I told him, "Well, you have given me the answer. This year, you will not get the RPPD. Next year, if you maintain an unbroken record [of payment], then at the end of that year, I will give you half of what you have lost here. So that is the incentive I'm giving to you. You are welcome to go and talk to CHC."' And the matter rested there.

The founders knew early on that if Asian Paints was to keep growing and indeed become an institution, then the organization would have to outlast all the them. The professionals had to be given the freedom to build an institution and a work culture they would be proud of. The experiment paid off beyond everyone's dreams. We are now in the year 2024. The first generation of founders passed away by the year 1997.

To think that Asian Paints has stayed number one for more than twenty-five years after that—run almost entirely by professionals—proves the strength of the work culture built assiduously by all the founders back in the 1950s and 1960s and continued consistently throughout. That culture has evolved and endured, and that is the difference between a boss being kind to his employees and an organization fostering care and cooperation as a culture.

Let us now end this chapter with an overview of where Asian Paints was when it became number one.

1960s: Manufacturing Grows in Volatile Times . . .

Asian Paints assumed leadership of the paints industry in very volatile times, by today's standards. In the 1960s, India fought two wars (one each with China and Pakistan) and saw the deaths of two prime ministers (Pandit Jawaharlal Nehru in 1964 and Pandit Lal Bahadur Shastri in 1966). Twin droughts in 1966 and 1967 hit foodgrain production and brought India on the verge of famine which was staved off by unprecedented food aid.[3] Foreign debt and foreign aid hit India's balance

[3] S.A. Aiyar, 'Drought Not a Big Calamity in India Anymore', *Times of India*, 29 July 2012, https://timesofindia.indiatimes.com/blogs/Swaminomics/drought-not-a-big-calamity-in-india-anymore/

of payments with foreign exchange reserves plummeting[4] to Rs 250 crore.

From FY1960–61 to FY1969–70, India's GDP growth averaged[5] just 4 per cent, including a contraction in GDP of 4 per cent in FY1965–66. During this period however, the manufacturing sector did relatively better, with growth averaging 6 per cent, and raising its overall share of GDP to 13 per cent in FY1969–70 compared to 11 per cent in FY1960–61. For perspective, agriculture's share reduced to 41 per cent from 48 per cent during the same period, reflecting the pain felt in the sector due to droughts.

With manufacturing and industry doing relatively well, the demand for paints continued to be strong. The paint panel of the Development Council for Oils, Soaps and Paints estimated the requirements of surface coating materials in 1966 at 1,60,000 tonnes—more than three times the 1961 output of 51,000 tonnes. This was a confident estimate since the third five-year plan stated[6] that the paint-consuming industries and construction activities had large expansion programmes in the Third Plan. Some of these bold forecasts would have come true given that the construction sector averaged growth of 6 per cent during FY1965–66 to FY1969–70, compared to 4 per cent for the manufacturing sector—both sectors growing faster on average than overall GDP whose growth was impacted by the agricultural sector.

. . . and Asian Paints Reaches #1 in 1967

Asian Paints benefited from the growth in industries and construction because the 1960s was the era of transformation for the company. In the previous two chapters, we have detailed

---

[4] 1965–66 Economic Survey, Part 1.

[5] Data, Ministry of Statistics and Program Implementation, Government Of India, n.d., https://www.mospi.gov.in/data, accessed on 7 January 2024.

[6] Appendix III(C), *Indian Paints Association* book, 1989.

how Asian Paints built up capabilities in production technology and R&D and ramped up distribution across India through innovative products and building franchises in the dealer community. The total of all their efforts is evident in Table 5.1.

Table 5.1: Asian Paints in the 1960s

	Sales		Profits		Total assets
	Rs (lakh)	per cent	Rs (lakh)	per cent	Rs (lakh)
1962	185		7		82
1963	230	24	8	16	88
1964	261	14	7	–7	95
1965	282	8	10	46	110
1966	362	28	13	23	137
1967	453	25	15	16	182
1968	553	22	21	42	220
1969	661	20	22	3	271
1970	809	22	23	6	280
1971	942	16	25	8	272

(Source: Asian Paints Annual Report 1971.)

When Asian Paints became number one in 1967, it was a twenty-five-year-old company. By hiring trained chemical engineers at their Bhandup factory, the first generation of founders had overcome their own lack of expertise in paint production technology.

By personally reaching out to smaller dealers and launching indigenously made innovative products, Asian Paints had created a credible franchise, convincing the dealers that they understood the market better than the competition. All this was great, but what next? Reaching the number one spot was a major achievement, but the road ahead had three challenges:

a) **Widening and deepening distribution:** Asian Paints was successful in building its brand franchise by going directly to dealers in rural areas. Larger institutional distributors in cities, who serviced the premium end of foreign brands, were also slowly coming on board. To sustain this momentum, branches had to be added and strengthened across India and new dealers had to be added and serviced. The founders could place chemists in their labs in Bhandup, but to find driven and motivated people willing to head branches across India and aggressively expand Asian Paints among the large dealers was the first challenge.
b) **Reducing dependency on debt and ramping up free cash flows:** Funding was no longer the problem that it was in the initial stages. Banks and financial institutions were more than willing to fund the #1 paints company in India. The next challenge would be to improve the working capital cycle by building a system that was better than the competition, leading to a reduction in debtor and inventory cycles.
c) **Establishing the brand:** Asian Paints was well known in India and it had even started to export small quantities (1971 exports were Rs 36 lakh out of gross sales of Rs 9 crore). Its product line was established with innovations like washable distemper, deeper shades of colours and small tins. Asian Paints had moved ahead of the competition that was still focused on industrial applications and premium, high-end paints. A strong mascot in the form of Gattu also helped. But Gattu was a corporate brand—the next challenge would be to reach the customer directly and make its paints (Apcolite, Tractor, etc.) into brands and slowly move up the value chain. This challenge would require marketing and advertising skills.

Accordingly, Champakbhai and the founders of Asian Paints decided to hire professional managerial talent, i.e., MBAs from IIMs. In doing this, the founders scored two major goals—comprehensively addressing all three challenges outlined above and creating and grooming a large pool of talent that would first provide valuable support to the second generation and eventually run the entire company. This was institution-building at its best. It came with many challenges, as we will see in the coming chapters, but it was a bold decision that would prove to be far-sighted.

Part 3

Racing Ahead

Chapter 6

Managing Growth

'Success in business is all about people, people, people. Whatever industry a company is in, its employees are its biggest competitive advantage.'

—Richard Branson

Asian Paints is renowned for professional management and, so far, we have discussed how Champakbhai and the founders hired people like Madhukar and Chari from outside the families and community and gave them room to grow as managers. For a brief history of the study of management and the birth of the IIMs, refer to Appendix 2. In this chapter, we discuss how Champakbhai and the founders weren't just at the right place at the right time. They were willing to bet on a novel concept in India much ahead of their peers and, as usual, they were proven right.

The Challenge of Professionals in a Family Business . . .

In my conversations with ex-employees and the Choksey family, one of my main questions was why the founders looked at recruiting from IIMs at a time when they had already reached the number one spot. The next generation was on its way. There was a credible second line of defence in Madhukar, Chari, etc. to keep operations running. The second generation was a large pool of talent given that there were four families, with each family having at least one child.

That alone meant there would be at least four young men willing to take the company to the next stage of growth, and the founders were still young (in their fifties) with enough time and motivation to guide their sons. The founders had tasted success with the chemists but it's one thing to have chemists run laboratories; setting up a cadre of MBAs to drive the next phase of growth would mean trusting young strangers with managing important parts of the company. It seemed like an experiment that could go either way. There were three challenges:

First, establishing trust between the family and the MBAs[1] would take time and could disrupt the existing system that had delivered spectacular results, namely propelling Asian Paints to number one in 1967.

Second, unlike family that is bound by blood, young MBAs are driven by career progress and salary. They could just leave for the next high-paying job knowing that they could never become MD/CEO at Asian Paints, in that era. As it turned out, the first IIM MBAs hired at Asian Paints lasted less than five years.

Third, hiring MBAs would be expensive and could impact profit before tax (PBT) margins which had hovered in the 1960s at 11 per cent of gross sales. Employee remuneration is usually the next big item of expenditure in manufacturing companies after raw materials costs.

---

[1] Till 2018/2019, IIMs offered a diploma (PGDM: post graduate diploma in management) instead of a degree (MBA: master's in business administration). More here: Somdatta Basu, 'IIM-Calcutta Set to Award Degrees for the First Time,' *Times of India*, 21 March 2019, https://timesofindia.indiatimes.com/city/kolkata/iim-c-set-to-award-degrees-for-the-first-time/articleshow/68505352.cms. For the sake of simplicity in this book, IIM MBAs also refer to IIM PGDM.

. . . Versus the Opportunities

Against these challenges were the opportunities and some threats. The MBAs could significantly widen Asian Paints' reach, improve product awareness and work to connect Asian Paints with dealers and customers on the ground. As Professor Roy writes,[2] this was the era when consumer goods were controlled by the bottom-up: wholesalers judged the market and sent feedback. The manufacturer's own sales team performed a monitoring function rather than dealing with consumers directly.

Thus, in the 1960s, the Bhandup factory produced what the dealers wanted; so, if a dealer in Pune wanted ten tins of red paint, the factory's job was to make it. On-the-ground intelligence, marketing, logistics, etc. had still not developed fully in the 1960s. Even with rudimentary systems, Asian Paints reached number one by identifying and filling up gaps that the competition could not provide using a direct-to-dealer approach that the competition missed out.

But the competition could easily replicate everything Asian Paints did and overtake them soon. Asian Paints needed to build significant moats. With a strong marketing and sales function, dealer relationships could be strengthened, brands could be built, and Asian Paints would be in control of what to sell, when to sell and where to sell, and hence stay ahead of the competition. These would constitute significant moats.

Fast-moving consumer goods (FMCG) companies like Hindustan Unilever (then Hindustan Lever) were already hiring professional managers as were some other paints companies. Bringing in MBAs would also professionalize the branches of the company. So, if Madhukar and Chari were effectively the second

---

[2] Professor Tirthankar Roy, *A Business History of India* (2018), Chapter 7, Box 7.4, Cambridge University Press 2018.

line of management after the founders at the Mumbai office, they needed to decentralize and give branches more autonomy—for which you needed qualified personnel. On balance, therefore, the opportunities outweighed the challenges. The death of Vakil in 1960 also had an impact on the founders, grimly reminding them of the uncertainty that accompanies a sudden departure and the risks of concentration of management at the top.

David Ogilvy famously said, 'If you always hire people who are smaller than you are, we shall become a company of dwarfs. If, on the other hand, you always hire people who are bigger than you are, we shall become a company of giants.' Atul Choksey recalls a variant of the line said by his father and told me, 'Champakbhai always believed in hiring people who were smarter than him.' Hence, the choice to go to the IIMs made sense to the founders.

The Journey Begins at IIMA

IIMA was founded in 1961 and the first batch of students started in 1964. The first batch consisted of forty-eight PGPs (Postgraduate Programme in Business Administration), as they were known then. Gold medallists included Diwan Arun Nanda (founder of the ad agency, Rediffusion) and the late management guru C.K. Prahalad.

In 1968, Champakbhai and Madhukar arrived at the iconic IIMA campus to recruit the first employees from IIM Ahmedabad for Asian Paints. Around 2000 km due east, IIM Calcutta (now Kolkata) had also started its first batch in 1964. Asian Paints founders were Gujaratis and it was probably the familiarity of Ahmedabad and the proximity to Mumbai that made the founders choose IIMA instead of IIMC as its first hunting ground. IIMC would also follow later.

Biji Kurien—The First Gold Medallist from IIMA to Join

In the third week of March 1968, an anxious twenty-eight-year-old final-year PGDM student checked in his pigeonhole mailbox at IIM Ahmedabad for any communication. The campus was buzzing with his batchmates discussing their interviews with companies who had come to select candidates and make offers. The twenty-seven-year-old man was Biji Kurien, one of two hires that Asian Paints made from IIMA. Kurien was an engineering graduate who had worked at Esso Standard Eastern (a subsidiary of Standard Oil New Jersey, USA, now ExxonMobil). He was one of eighty-three PGPs in the batch of 1968[3]—the third batch at IIMA. The convocation was on 13 April 1968 and Kurien was running out of time.

Kurien's curriculum vitae (CV) was part of the placement office's master register for the recruiters even though he had not applied for any of the vacancies on offer. With two years of work experience at a multinational and now with an MBA degree, Kurien found that the recruiters at IIMA either didn't have the job or the salary that he wanted, hence he had not applied specifically for any offer. But as luck would have it, his CV had been noticed.

He found a note from the placement office in his pigeonhole saying that the chairman and the executive director of Asian Paints, 'a company no one had heard of at that time', were on the campus and would like to meet him in the afternoon. Champakbhai and Madhukar had come in the morning and since not many PGPs had applied for the Asian Paints job, they had only a few CVs. They went through the master register containing all CVs of the PGPs and picked up a few, including Kurien's, that they found interesting.

The interview went well and when the key question of salary expectations came up, Biji asked for Rs 1200 per month, since his last drawn salary at Esso, two years earlier, was Rs 860/ month. A week later, Biji got a job offer from Asian Paints. The backstory is interesting because Champakbhai and Madhukar thought the salary expectations were too high, given that other candidates were asking for Rs 750 per month.

---

[3] Bhavesh Patel, '3rd Convocation @ Archives', n.d., https://archives.iima.ac.in/convocation/3rd-Convocation.html, accessed on 7 January 2024.

Chairman of the Placement Committee, Professor G.R. Kulkarni, had convinced Champakbhai and Madhukar to hire Kurien since he would be the topper of the batch (then Prime Minister Indira Gandhi was chief guest at the convocation and handed over the gold medal to Kurien a few weeks later) and companies were offering even higher salaries than Rs750/month. Kurien joined Asian Paints on 2 May 1968 and remained till 1972 when he joined British Paints (later known as Berger Paints) and went on to become CEO in 1980 and left in 1994. After that, Kurien set up his own consultancy and has been working with companies and the paints industry.

I met Kurien in Chennai for the second time after first meeting him in 2015 for *The Unusual Billionaires*. Remembering how he chose to join Asian Paints, he told me, 'Campus interviews in those days were still an unknown concept. Companies would send managers to choose from the candidates. And here was this company that sent both the chairman and executive director to IIMA!'

Kurien joined the head office at Bombay where he handled industrial sales. 'They [Asian Paints] hired from IIMA not just to hire people outside their friends, family and community, but also to look at new things. So, for example, I told them they didn't need to stick to making only what everyone else made. I gave them the idea of manufacturing specialized resins,' he told me.

T.N. Ramaswamy—Candidate #2 from IIMA

The second hire from IIMA was T.N. Ramaswamy. After graduating from Madras University with a B.Com degree, Mr Ramaswamy went straight to IIM Ahmedabad. He worked for five years at Asian Paints (1968 to 1973), mainly at the Mumbai office first (Das Chambers near the Bombay Stock Exchange), and then at Nirmal Building at Nariman Point.

Although basically a finance person, his role extended beyond finance and into other areas where number crunching and analysis were involved, such as marketing services and planning.

After a five-year stint, Ramaswamy left Asian Paints to move overseas. He first worked for the Mehta Group in East Africa for twelve years and then in various countries and capacities for the Lakshmi N. Mittal-promoted global steel group for eighteen years. I spoke with Ramaswamy who is now based in Coimbatore about his interview and his stint at Asian Paints.

He told me,

> 'Mr Madhukar conducted my interview. Asian Paints was my first job, and I had no experience of corporate culture before that. My time at Asian Paints was a very good learning experience, giving me on-ground exposure to concepts of collaboration and teamwork—things that you don't learn at the institute. At Asian Paints, I developed an eye for efficiency, not in the theoretical way but in a practical way. Getting things done and delivering results was deeply ingrained in their culture right down to support staff. You don't see that very often. There was a lot of human touch as well. I joined as a raw beginner. In other companies, such fresh entrants rarely get access to the executive director or chairman, whereas here it was routine. I would run into them regularly,' he told me.

When I asked him about Champakbhai, Ramaswamy told me, 'Champakbhai stood tall, both literally and figuratively. He was a leader but without an authoritarian approach. He had a firm grasp on all business matters, and brought his vision and wisdom to all decisions. He was very articulate, and every sentence was carefully considered.'

Doubling Down on the IIM Bet

After hiring Kurien and Ramaswamy, Asian Paints doubled down on its bet. Even though both employees left within five years, the organization kept hiring from IIMA. Chinmay Tumbe, associate professor of Economics at IIMA and member of the IIMA Archives Committee, told me that in the first decade of IIMA, Asian Paints was the fifth-largest recruiter at thirteen (number of MBAs recruited from IIMA). The first four were Larsen & Toubro (twenty-four), Hindustan Unilever (nineteen), First National City Bank (now Citibank, nineteen) and TELCO (now Tata Motors, fifteen).

In doing this, it was the only family-held and family-run (Tata Group companies were headed by professionals) company, the only paints company, and one of just three Indian companies (HUL and Citibank were multinationals) to hire professional talent in large numbers from IIMA.

In 1968, Professor Kulkarni recommended Champakbhai and Madhukar to hire Kurien. By the 1980s, this had reversed. Bharat Puri recalled how the legendary IIMA professor, Labdhi Bhandari had told him to join Asian Paints. 'I had many offers, but Professor Bhandari told me that if I wanted to learn, I should go to Asian Paints. It was a Day 1 company and had a history as a learning organization,' Puri told me, adding, 'Champakbhai Choksey was very clear that MBAs add value.'

Another way of understanding Asian Paints' commitment to hiring MBAs (first from IIMs and then across the best B-Schools in the country), back in the 1970s and 1980s, is to consider that the company would assign the task of campus hiring to a few senior management personnel (like Chari, Khan, Abraham, Murty, etc.). 'The same team would visit all the campuses, and during hiring season, they spent most of their time on this activity as it was seen to be vital for the company's future. And it worked, we got many talented people who moved to leadership roles within and outside Asian Paints,' V.S. Ram, ex-CEO of Asian PPG Industries and an Asian Paints veteran, told me. While the early MBAs started in sales and marketing, they would eventually proliferate across functions like finance, computers, production planning, etc. as we see in the next few chapters. Many of them would return as recruiters to the same IIMs they were recruited from.

The Indian CEO Factory

In his 2019 book, *The CEO Factory*, Sudhir Sitapati, who spent twenty-two years at HUL and is currently the CEO of Godrej Consumer Products, wrote that there were then around 400 HUL alumni who are CEOs/CXOs across corporate India, earning HUL the title 'the CEO Factory' in corporate circles. When I met Bharat Puri, he told me that he believed that Asian Paints was probably the Indian equivalent of the CEO Factory.

He rattled off many names, some of whom were his colleagues, bosses and juniors, who went on to become CEOs of famous brands. I worked on his claim and, with Bharat's extremely helpful assistance, could make a list of thirty such Asian Paints employees. This list names thirty individuals who worked at Asian Paints and went on to leadership positions at many organizations. Since the entire work experience cannot be summarized in this book, I have chosen one organization at random for each individual. Hence the list is just indicative and not exhaustive. For example, it excludes all three CEOs of Asian Paints—P.M. Murty, K.B.S. Anand and Amit Syngle. Moreover, some like Puri have been CEOs in other companies like Cadbury.

Table 6.1: Asian Paints—An Indian CEO Factory

	Name	Company
1	Ajit Mantagani	Arvind Limited
2	Amitav Sur	Berger Paints, Bahrain
3	Anurag Handa	Blowplast
4	A.S. Sundaresan	JSW Paints
5	Bharat Puri	Pidilite
6	Biji Kurien	Berger Paints
7	Chandramouli Venkatesan	Mondelez (previously Cadbury)
8	Kartik Kaushik	Citibank

9	K.S. Narayanan	McCain
10	P.G. Ponnapa	AOL India
11	Prabhakar Jain	Goodyear
12	Rajiv Chandra	Reckitt Benckiser
13	Rajiv Garodia	Western Union
14	Ravi Karamcheti	Kodak India
15	Rohit Aggarwal	Huntsman Textiles
16	Sanjay Purohit	Sapphire Foods
17	Sanjeev Aga	Idea Cellular
18	Subir Bose	Berger Paints
19	T.L. Palani Kumar	New Holland Tractors
20	Venkatesh Kini	The Coca-Cola Company
21	Vijay Jayaram	Blowplast
22	Vipul Prakash	DFM Foods
23	Vivek Subramaniam	Pidlite (CEO, Fevicol)
24	Anoop Hoon	Century Plyboards
25	R. Ramakrishnan	Polycab
26	Vamsi Mohan Thati	The Coca-Cola Company
27	Deepak Mehrotra	Ashirvad Pipes
28	Uday Shankar Sinha	PepsiCo
29	Jagdish Acharya	PPG Asian Paints
30	Jaideep Nandi	Bajaj Consumer Care

(Source: With help and guidance from Bharat Puri. Data is from LinkedIn and other[4] websites. Note: 1) The companies mentioned are only one of others where the individual has worked; 2) Designation might not specifically be 'CEO' but is indicative of seniority in position)

[4] Amitav Sur, https://prabook.com/web/amitav.sur/343584, accessed 5 January 2024.

A Transition and a Purge

With the hiring of the first MBAs in 1968, Asian Paints had begun a slow but firm transition towards being a professionally run company. This was not an easy transition since a small old guard had to be eased out. Like any large family-run company, Asian Paints employees also included a few who were related to the founding families or were friends or came via references within the family. While there were also hard-working senior staff like Madhukar, Chari, Abraham, etc. this was still a family-owned and family-run business run the traditional way.

'We had to fend for ourselves and handle people who had been working there for a long time. There was some resistance, but that was to be expected since people were promoted to a managerial level after they performed at lower levels but we [the new MBAs] just walked in,' Biji Kurien told me. For MBAs to fit in, an entirely new culture would need to evolve for the experiment to be a success. And this culture was obviously in contrast to the professional and meritocratic atmosphere that the MBAs expected.

Some practices were basic and led more by default or a lack of better ideas than anything else; some because owners could not trust employees at far-flung branches in an era without mobile telephones or the Internet. As Kurien writes in his book, he sees these practices even today at branches of private companies, partnerships, proprietorship firms, etc. For example, when Kurien took over the Madras branch, to his surprise, he found that expense reimbursements took ten to twenty days and in some cases weren't even reimbursed by the company. Expenses on tea offered to dealers who visited the branch benefited the employee but not the company and hence were not reimbursable. Biji professionalized the process, asked for a rational allocation of money for expenditure, and set up a separate bank account for expenses for reimbursements. This practice was then adopted for other branches too—improving payment time but more importantly, improving transparency as well.

In the coming decade, a broad purge of inefficient employees got underway, with the implicit approval of Champakbhai. And ex-employee told me,

> 'He said be fair and reasonable about it. If someone you want to let go asks for three months' or six months' notice period give him that time. If he requires some assistance, give that to him. For example, if someone wants to become a painting contractor, talk to a dealer and get him attached; tell the dealer to take care of that person. Do not give [the people who have to be let go] any money, instead give them contacts. But they must leave. The time has come because these people will impede the organization.'

Dishonesty was not to be tolerated under any circumstances and employees caught being dishonest were to be sacked on the spot without any approvals from the family, he said, and went on to add that in that era, he had personally fired many such people, including employees related to/hired via the reference of the family. This was the level of commitment that Champakbhai and the founders had to make Asian Paints into an institution.

I met P.M. Murty (mentioned in the previous chapter) in Hyderabad. Mr Murty is an IIMC alumnus and joined Asian Paints in 1971. He had retired as the head of the decorative business of the organization but was called back to become the first professional managing director and CEO of Asian Paints in 2008 or 2009. He finally retired in 2012, after spending forty years at Asian Paints. Like Chari, Murty has seen three generations of promoter families. He said,

> 'Champakbhai yearned for a modern company. He was willing to spend money and back the right people for his vision. He never imposed his views. If you were willing to try

something radical, he would tell you to try. He was looking for passionate people and was willing to back them to the hilt. If you're not passionate, of if you are always dependent on your boss to tell you what to do, then you won't get too far—that was Champakbhai's belief.'

It was precisely this meritorious culture that would be built first by Champakbhai and the founders, assisted by the next line of defence (Madhukar, Chari, Abraham, Jhaveri and Trivedi), and then eventually the MBAs that followed, that would eventually transition Asian Paints from a family-owned business to a professionally run company with a great work culture.

Chapter 7

A Mainframe at Bhandup

'Computers are incredibly fast, accurate, and stupid. Human beings are incredibly slow, inaccurate, and brilliant. Together they are powerful beyond imagination.'

—Albert Einstein

Asian Paints achieved significant efficiencies with its early investment in computers. In this chapter, we look at the man responsible for the early gains and how the first mainframe was integrated within the company at Bhandup. For a better understanding of the history of computers in India, please read Appendix 3 before you begin reading this chapter.

From Salem to Bhandup

Gattu had an unexpected pay-off for Asian Paints in a way that Champakbhai or the founders of Asian Paints could never have imagined. In the 1960s, a young boy living near Salem, a large city about 350 km from Chennai in the southern state of Tamil Nadu, flipped through a railway timetable at home. His father was a stationmaster for Southern Railways, so a timetable was always handy at home.

He saw an ad for a paints company featuring Gattu, and the name 'Asian Paints' stayed in his head. The boy went on to do his graduation in electrical engineering from PSG College of

Technology in Coimbatore, another large city in Tamil Nadu. After his graduation, he joined Madras State Electricity Board,[1] where he worked for a year. Unlike many of his generation, for whom a government job was a dream, the boy, now a young man, wanted to join the private sector.

He had seen an ad for IIMA when he had visited Madras University for some work. IIMA was not well known at that time, but he thought it was worth the risk. He was admitted to the fourth batch[2] of IIMA and graduated in 1969, with a gold medal.

Madhukar interviewed him and the man was selected for a job at Asian Paints. That young man's name is V. Veeraraghavan, and he would go on to lead the computer revolution at Asian Paints. 'I was a gamble for Asian Paints. They put Kurien in marketing but in my case, they took me for computers before knowing what are computers,' Veeraraghavan told me. Veeraraghavan is known affectionately as Veera among his colleagues, at least two of whom told me that Veera was the best boss they had when they were working at Asian Paints.

Freshly recruited MBAs went through an induction and training process in Mumbai after which they would be allotted their assignments. Kurien, for example, went to the Chennai Branch, whereas Ramaswamy stayed in the finance function in Mumbai. There was no induction or training for Veeraraghavan. He joined on 2 May 1969, was thrown in the deep end and told to swim. His job was to figure out how to use computers at Asian Paints. But how popular were computers in India in 1969?

Asian Paints—IBM or ICL?

For Veeraraghavan in the early 1970s, there were two choices—the IBM 1401 or the ICL 1901A. 'By that time, the IBM 1401

---

[1] Known today as Tamil Nadu Generation and Distribution Corporation Limited, or TANGEDCO.

[2] Bhavesh Patel, '4th Convocation @ Archives', https://archives.iima.ac.in/convocation/4th-Convocation.html, accessed on 5 January 2024.

had already become obsolete, and we could not import the IBM 360, which was next in line. So, we chose the ICL 1901A.' Asian Paints' first computer was the ICL 1901A which was purchased for Rs 30 lakh, from what Veeraraghavan told me. He said,

> 'I wrote to Chari in late 1970 or early 1971 suggesting that we should buy the computer. Chari forwarded the letter to the partners who approved it. The matter was discussed with Champakbhai, Bipinbhai [Jhaveri], Kishan and Abraham. Looking back now, I am surprised how the decision was taken on faith and the belief that a computer strategy would work out. It took two years for the computer to be delivered. I think it arrived in 1972 or 1973 because, by mid-1975, I clearly recall that we had started using the computer.'

Since there was a long waiting period till the computer arrived, Veeraraghavan remembers using punch cards and unit recording machines at a third-party vendor to process data. Branches took two to three weeks to send their data to Mumbai. Asian Paints had around twenty products but about 750 stock-keeping units (SKUs) with Apcolite and Tractor being the most important ones, each having more than 100 SKUs (various colours, various pack sizes, etc.). 'By the 20th of every month, we would have all the dealer data from across India which would then be punched into cards which were fed into unit recording machines for the output,' Veeraraghavan told me.

Asian Paints was already using data processing capabilities before the computer came in—and this is consistent with the history of computers in corporate India. Maybe, having an illustrious neighbour in the form of Tata Consultancy Services (TCS) helped Asian Paints make the decision.

The Mainframe Arrives at Bhandup

Real estate at Bhandup is cheaper than Nariman Point so it was an obvious decision for Asian Paints to install the computer at the Bhandup plant in a separate building when it arrived in the early 1970s. Things got off to a slow start and the computer was a 'low-key affair'. When it was ready, Veeraraghavan told me how the operation worked at the Bhandup building.

'There were six system executives [including Veeraraghavan and K. Srinivasan who was also an engineer and MBA], eight programmers, twelve punch machine operators, and around six computer operators. We hired staff from outside for the computer, but we also trained existing employees to work with the computer,' he told me.

Data from the field would arrive at Bhandup in the evening at around 5–5.30 p.m. after which the punch operators would punch the data into cards—the most manually intensive part of the job—till around 11 p.m. After this, the cards would be fed into the system by the computer operators who worked the night shift. The output from the mainframe would be out by around 4 a.m. in the form of tapes from which reports would be printed. By 7 a.m., the computer output would be ready for distribution.

The initial beneficiaries were the Bombay and Thane areas for Asian Paints since these were nearest to Bhandup. For branches and dealers across India, especially those in far-flung areas, data would take more time to arrive and hence the benefits took longer to accrue. 'In roughly one year, we had a system of all the branches reporting their stocks and their estimated sales coming into HQ [Bhandup factory] once every fifteen days. We matched this with production at the factory; for example, Apcolite white would be packed in 50 ml tins or 100 ml tins, etc. for most of the high-selling products. We used data instead of gut feel,' Veeraraghavan told me.

He added,

> 'After a few years, we could respond within twelve hours—that is to say, feedback from the field today would reflect in the factory's operations the next morning. So, we could align the factory's production both as per the intelligence gleaned from the computer's output and managerial feedback,

and allot and dispatch stocks to branches based on demand. The bottom line was that there would be instructions on what had to be packed and where [which bay for which city] it had to be placed on the next day. The truck just had to pick up the goods and deliver them. That was the foundation of our strengths in supply chain management.'

Huge Gains in Inventory Management

Inventory was the first target for the computer since that was the most critical component of working capital. Stocks at the branch were reduced significantly. The results took time but were dramatic. Inventory (as day sales) dipped to fifty-eight days in 1980 from 107 days in 1970. These were still the early days of computers at Asian Paints and the benefits would accrue only over time and many more system upgrades. But the foundation of Asian Paints' pioneering efforts in IT systems—regarded as the best in the paints industry—was laid by the ICL 1901A mainframe bought by the founders in the early 1970s.

Working Capital Management as a Competitive Advantage

Working capital is the lifeblood of a company. It is literally the capital with which the company works on a day-to-day basis. It is the difference between current assets (mainly debtors and inventory) and current liabilities (mainly creditors and provisions). If a company keeps waiting for money from their debtors to pay up or for their inventory to sell, they will need to borrow money to pay rent, salaries of employees and other major costs. If these borrowings go out of control, a company runs the risk of falling into a debt trap. However, if a company cracks the working capital cycle and can reduce the time taken from debtors to pay or inventory to sell, it has easy access to fund its day-to-day expenditure. There are sectors, like FMCG, where this is easy and there are sectors, like infrastructure, where this is difficult.

Asian Paints broke away from other paints companies with its open market policy (Chapter 3). With its investment in computers in the 1970s, it was able to service these dealers much better. With the RPPD (discussed later in this chapter), it was able to get funds quicker from them. This boosted Asian Paints' free cash flows and turned working capital management into a competitive advantage for the company as well as an industry standard in India Inc.

Describing the dealer network in its full glory, Saurabh Mukherjea, in 2019, wrote on the Marcellus Blog,[3]

> 'Behind this remarkable network architected by Champaklal Choksey, is fifty years of proprietary data on paint demand for each neighbourhood in India, for every hour of the day, for every day of the year. That allows Asian Paints to forecast your paint demand just like Amazon can second guess what you will buy when you visit their website next. Asian Paints' proprietary data, its forecasting ability and its distribution network give it a working capital cycle of eight days. Nobody else in the paint sector comes remotely close to Asian Paints on this metric. As a result, Asian Paints ROCE (usually at around 30 per cent) and free cash flows are head and shoulders above its rivals.'

Putting the Cost of the Mainframe into Perspective

How much was the investment in the mainframe (Rs 30 lakh) for Asian Paints back in the early 1970s? Asian Paints' gross block was Rs 1.8 crore in 1972 and its total assets were around Rs 3 crore. And by 1972, Asian Paints for the very first time, crossed sales of Rs 10 crore. So Rs 30 lakh works out to about a fifth of the gross block and a tenth of the total assets—a reasonably large bet.

---

[3] Saurabh Mukherjea, Marcellus, https://marcellus.in/blogs/marcellus-unusual-billionaires-flip-the-competitive-paradigm/, June 2019.

For perspective, here is how S. Mahalingam, then CFO of TCS, recalls[4] importing the top-of-the-line IBM 3090 in the 1980s: 'At that time the gross block [worth of an asset] of the IBM 3090 was going to be larger than the total gross block [of all the other computers put together] of TCS.' Obviously, there is a difference between an IT firm taking a disproportionately huge bet on buying an asset they knew of, versus a paints company betting on an asset that they did not know how to use, and for which they had hired an IIMA gold medallist who was not even related to the families of the promoters in any way. By all counts, it was an audacious bet and a leap of faith for Champakbhai and the founders, and one that would pay off slowly but spectacularly over the long term.

How much is Rs 30 lakh worth today? That would depend on the rate of inflation assumed for fifty years (1973 to 2023); at 5 per cent inflation Rs 30 lakh in 1973 would be worth Rs 3.4 crore today. At a higher inflation rate of 8 per cent, it would be worth Rs 8.8 crore today.

The RPPD—Another Innovation for the Dealers

Another significant breakthrough for Asian Paints during this era was the famous regular payment performance discount (RPPD) which was a switch from the cash discount being followed by the company. Veeraraghavan told me, 'The RPPD, and many other things like managing working capital, could not have been effectively implemented without the strength and power of the computerized systems.'

Asian Paints then offered forty-five days (from the date of invoice) to all retailers and up to sixty days to the larger retailers. To induce faster payments, retailers were offered a 1.5 per cent cash discount if they paid within twenty-one days. The system

[4] 'Itihaasa', https://itihaasa.com/describe/sartefact/001_001_0394?term=Import+of+IBM+3090+by+TCS&sf=1, accessed on 6 January 2024.

wasn't working as well as the founders wanted. Retailers availed of the discount whenever they wanted and dragged payment of invoices beyond forty-five days (after which supplies were halted till dues were cleared) and in some cases beyond ninety days after buying materials from Asian Paints. A small group of MBAs (like Biji Kurien and Amitav Sur, who was Veeraraghavan's batchmate from IIMA, etc.) was approached to devise a new scheme.

The group came with the RPPD which offered a 2.5 per cent[5] discount for payments made within thirty days—thus extending the period of credit (from twenty-one days) and raising the rate of discount (1.5 per cent). Thus, the discount shifted from being a cash discount (which was deducted from the dealer's invoice and hence the dealer paid the net amount) to a payment discount (which would be paid out by Asian Paints and hence the dealer paid the full invoice amount).

But there were riders to this, namely a) payment had to be credited to the Asian Paints bank account within thirty days, and b) payments had to be made consistently throughout the year. If the retailer missed even one invoice, he would not be considered for the scheme, and c) since RPPD was a payment discount which would be credited at the end of the accounting year, rebate credit notes would continue so as to provide liquidity to the dealer during the year.

Kurien writes about four advantages to the scheme, namely a) the onus of prompt payments shifted to the retailer; b) Asian Paints could forecast cash flow better; c) retailers got better and more uniform prices versus other dealers; and d) Asian Paints sales staff could focus on sales instead of collections. In *The Unusual Billionaires*, Saurabh Mukherjea writes about how RPPD also ensured that the smaller retailers of Asian Paints got a better deal than the channel (dealers, distributors, etc.) employed by larger multinational companies that enjoyed 180 days of credit, which

[5] In his book, *The Unusual Billionaires*, Saurabh Mukherjea quotes a slightly different version, namely 3.5 per cent RPPD.

could even extend to one year in some cases, at a time when capital was expensive for retailers.

Expanding Horizons beyond IIMA

Champakbhai and the founders thus hired MBAs from IIMA and sent them directly to the core areas that mattered most, namely branch sales, computers and working capital.

In 1971, the first MBAs from IIMC were hired, namely Munir M. Khan and P.M. Murty—both of whom were sent for training to Kurien. From here on, hiring from IIMs and other B-Schools became annual affairs so that by the end of the 1970s, there was a sizeable cadre of MBAs working at Asian Paints. With Madhukar leaving the firm, the job of hiring from the IIMs would pass on to Chari, and eventually the MBAs themselves would go to the campus to recruit. For example, V.S. Ram (IIMC batch of 1974, who would go on to head the Asian Paints PPG venture) was recruited by M.M. Khan.

The early impact of MBAs on Asian Paints is hard to measure in numbers since their real impact was to create a meritocratic environment and a professional company—benefits which cannot be measured in financial statements. But even if one saw the financial results (refer to Table 7.1), there was a noticeable shift in the quality of cash flows, with the core operations being the key driver for funding capital expenditure.

This is how high-quality companies operate versus those that need constant external funding like loans or dilutions in equity and whose cash flows are then mostly spent on paying interest and repaying loans or on funding large working-capital cycles. Asian Paints' capital efficiencies remained high even during the exorbitant corporate tax regimes of 65–70 per cent during the 1960s and 1970s.

Veeraraghavan went from heading systems to heading the Bhandup factory in 1978, a job he took over from Munir Khan. Rotating MBAs around different operational areas (marketing, sales, factory, etc.) was first faced with resistance

Table 7.1: Asian Paints, sources and applications of fund, cumulative 1974 to 1980

(Rs in lakh)	1974–1980 (total)
Inflows	
Profit after tax (adding back depreciation)	804
Increase in borrowing	43
Investments sold	34
Write back of provisions and tax refunds	44
Total inflows	**926**
Capital expenditure	–617
Dividends paid	–236
Increase in working capital	–74
Total outflows	**–927**

(Source: Annual reports)

(from the MBAs) and then over the long term made routine at Asian Paints. 'Working with the company was fun, there was tremendous scope to do what you wanted to do. There was pressure [to perform] but at the end of the day, there was no force,' Veeraraghavan told me.

Veeraraghavan left Asian Paints as the head of the Bhandup plant in 1982 after spending thirteen years in the company, including the installation of the ICL 1901A.

Recalling his days at Asian Paints, he told me, 'CHC was anything but conventional. He used psychology as a weapon to change the company.' He recalled that while building the Ankleshwar plant, Champakbhai had said that no one from Bhandup would be transferred to Ankleshwar. He wanted a quantum jump in the new plant versus the older plant. There were teething problems, and while Chari made the effort, the driving force was Champakbhai. Eventually, Ankleshwar turned out to be a success. Veeraraghavan recalled Champakbhai saying, 'All of you have got it wrong. You build a factory with good people. So, you need to make the people comfortable there. What are we doing about that? Put a person who enjoys his job there, do everything else later.' This approach resonated with me in recollections made by Pramesh Khanna, Jagdish Acharya and V.S. Ram, all of whom spent significant time in overseas operations.

Making people comfortable at their jobs sounded strange at that time when the obvious approach was to use people who had already set up the Bhandup plant to set up the Ankleshwar plant. 'At that time, we didn't understand or appreciate what CHC said. Then he told us a story of people crossing the river and how some of them slip and some make it through. We couldn't understand that but obviously since he was saying it, there had to be meaning,' Veeraraghavan told me with a smile.

He asked Abraham who translated it for him. It meant that only the strongest and the most flexible would cross the river without difficulty. One inference was that in a temporary situation where costs had risen, the paints company that did not increase prices would slip into the river. 'CHC used many such examples that made no sense to us immediately but would be implemented with great success,' Veeraraghavan told me.

Veeraraghavan's wife, Lakshmi, was sitting with us when I met them in March 2023 in Bengaluru. While she never interacted directly with Champakbhai, she reminisced about many visits to the nearby Nirmal office at Nariman Point (just across the road from LIC's HQ). 'We used to go to the Asian Paints office for *chopda pujan* on Diwali, when they worship the accounts books for the Hindu New Year. We started buying gold or silver on Dhanteras after exposure to this culture,' she told me.

This reminded me of what Priya Bhumkar had said about values that endured at her firm from the time of her father-in-law's work at Asian Paints. Indeed, employees would continue to join and leave Asian Paints but at least for a few of them, Asian Paints never left the employees.

Family photo of the Chokseys with Champakbhai and his wife
Ashvinaben (both at the centre)
flanked by their children and the children's spouses
along with their grandchildren.

Champakbhai in his middle years.

Champakbhai in his later years.

Champakbhai and his wife Ashvinaben during younger days.

Sushilaben, also known as Sushilaba, Ashvinaben's sister and Champakbhai's aunt, who is spoken about in Chapter 2 of this book.

The founders of Asian Paints (from left to right): Champakbhai Choksey, Suryakantbhai Dani, Chimanbhai Choksi and Arvindbhai Vakil.

Champakbhai addressing a gathering.

Champakbhai and B.R. Trivedi.

Chapter 8

The Internal Emergency

'Adversity causes some men to break; others to break records.'
—William A. Ward

Entering the 1970s with a Health Setback

In December 1971, at the age of fifty-five and just one year after his second grandson Prashant was born, Champakbhai suffered a heart attack. The Choksey family still remembers the painful episode vividly. Amit Choksey recalled, 'It was very traumatic to see him in such a weak condition. Mummy was always after him to take care of himself. Fortunately, he survived without major damage.' Sunita Choksey (Girish's wife) recalled, 'It happened at home at night, and we immediately called for the ambulance and went to Bombay Hospital. Doctors told us to wait and watch for seventy-two hours and eventually, he recovered. His family was his full-time priority, and he was always a very strong man.'

Rita Parekh—The Closest to Champakbhai

Even though Champakbhai returned to work after a few months, eventually he would require a bypass surgery. 'We found who was the best surgeon in this field. At that time, it was Dr Denton

Cooley[1] so we went to St Luke's Hospital in Houston in 1988 and had the procedure done,' Atul Choksey told me.

Among the four children, Rita Parekh (nee Choksey), affectionately known as 'Daggi', was the closest to her father. Her marriage to Ashok Parekh in 1966, just two years before Asian Paints became #1 in the paints industry, was the first in the Choksey family. Ashok Parekh was senior president at Grasim Industries and instrumental in setting up its chemical division[2] in Nagda, Madhya Pradesh.

Within the Choksey family, Rita is regarded as the closest to Champakbhai not only in terms of love and affection but also in terms of personality, especially strength. 'Rita-ben is Papa. She is another Champakbhai. She was always strong and is even stronger now,' Parul, Atul's wife, told me. Atul told me, 'She has the last word even today.'

Rita lost her husband, relatively early (when she was fifty-eight) and unexpectedly in 2001, just four years after losing Champakbhai. Behind her soft-spoken manner, there is a steely resolve and discipline, which she also picked up from her father. Having done a course in interior design, Rita would often go with Champakbhai to Geetanjali when the building was being constructed. As a child, she would tag along with Champakbhai to the old factory when she had school holidays.

For the bypass, Champakbhai insisted that Rita accompany him to the USA. Rita left her young daughters with Ashok and went to Houston. 'My father was everything to me. He made me courageous and taught me how to be organized and disciplined. He was not a diplomatic person but was open with everyone. In the early days, staff, workers and relatives could come home and meet him for any problem and he would courteously meet

---

[1] Wikipedia contributors, 'Denton Cooley,' Wikipedia, 8 August 2023, https://en.wikipedia.org/wiki/Denton_Cooley.

[2] 'Nagda',grasim.com,https://www.grasim.com/about-us/plants/nagda,accessed on 6 January 2024.

them, offering tea and snacks and promising to resolve their problems,' she told me.

Key Transitions in 1971

Thus, in 1971, Asian Paints had two key setbacks. First, in early 1971, Madhukar left the company to join Berger Paints (then British Paints) and in December 1971, Champakbhai had a heart attack. Yet, growth continued unabated (sales in 1972 were up 27 per cent and profits up 10 per cent). When Madhukar left, he was the executive director of the company and hence his departure created a major gap at the top. In 1971, there was a reorganization[3] with Chari moved to become general manager of the company and C.V. Abraham, the sales manager.

By the 1970s, the second generation was also entering the company and usually worked alongside a professional to learn the ropes at Asian Paints; for example, Girish Choksey worked with Abraham in marketing. While all three sons, namely Girish (in 1966), Atul (in 1973) and Amit (in 1977) joined Asian Paints, Atul stayed on, and Girish and Amit moved on later to their respective businesses.

Recalling his time there, Girish told me, 'I joined Asian Paints as an executive and was told to go by train to the Bhandup factory. I was just like anyone else on the staff and used to have lunch with everyone else. I started in the laboratory to learn how products were made and then moved to other areas like sales. I looked at industrial sales and managed to bag Godrej as a major customer then.' Amit told me, 'I was trained and sent across plants as well as branches to learn how they work. I knew that I would have to eventually move out of Asian Paints and so I needed to learn as much as possible.'

Transitions and succession planning are critical turning points in the history of companies. In the 1970s, there were thus

[3] Biji Kurien, *Half a Century and Still at the Crease* (2022).

four groups working simultaneously charting the future course at Asian Paints—first, the three founders who had entered their sixties; second, the original set of non-family professionals (Abraham, Chari, Jhaveri, Trivedi) who were well entrenched in their roles; third, the second generation who had joined in; and fourth, the continuing rush of young MBAs from B-Schools. The evolution of the next generation of leaders had begun.

Setting Separate Courses within Family

Champakbhai knew that the ambitions and aspirations of the next generation could become difficult to manage. The only way to keep everyone happy was to give them their own business to run, while Atul would stay at Asian Paints. In 1973, the Choksey family acquired Hindustan Mineral Products (today, HMP Minerals which makes specialty minerals) which would be led by Girish Choksey to run after he quit Asian Paints. When Amit Choksey left Asian Paints, he joined his brother at HMP in the late 1970s.

Within HMP, Amit started a new construction chemicals division which was hived off as Choksey Chemicals in 1985. In 1992, Amit acquired Mazda Colours which he has been running full-time ever since. Girish Choksey and his sons run HMP and Choksey Chemicals. All the companies are closely related to the chemicals and paints business, but as mentioned earlier, Asian Paints was a private limited company till 1982 and the concept of corporate governance and related party transactions was not as evolved in that era.

'Our father separated us in his presence. He always used to say that once you get married, the kitchen and the business should be separate and only then will you stay together and not step on each other's toes. You will have the best of relationships throughout your life—and that is exactly what happened,' Amit told me. He added, 'The next generation within the Choksey family also gets along well. We are independent and dependent at the same time. Of course, when he [Champakbhai] decided to separate us, it came as a shock to all of us. But he was right.'

Champakbhai's family philosophy of charting your own course outside of Asian Paints continued to the third generation as well. Prashant Choksey told me,

> 'I remember him talking with me and wondering how will the family progress and do things differently. His tenet was to lead a business or a venture on our own to realize and fulfil your capabilities; that is the only way to live together and not fight with anyone. He told me that Asian [Paints] is this giant cruise ship where there are enough smart people to navigate its course. So if I [Prashant] have to learn something, I will have to [go] somewhere else to be the entrepreneur I wanted to be.'

The Oil Shock Hits Home

India's Finance Minister Yashwantrao Chavan did not mince his words. On 28 February 1974, para 3 of his budget speech read as follows, 'I would like to state frankly that in the coming financial year, the economy will be faced with even greater challenges. Its strength and adaptability will be severely tested. The steep rise in the price of crude oil and also some other commodities has turned the terms of trade sharply against us and has rendered our tasks exceptionally difficult.'

In the previous year, the failure of monsoons had led to a severe drought. The oil crisis of the 1970s had raised oil prices globally. An embargo[4] by the Organization of Arab Petroleum Exporting Countries (OAPEC) on the United States of America drove a surge in crude oil prices. In the USA, oil prices quadrupled to $11.95/barrel in January 1974 from $2.90/barrel before the embargo.

Crude oil, as mentioned earlier, is a critical component of raw material prices for paints companies. India was reeling

[4] Michael Corbett, 'Oil Shock of 1973–74', Federal Reserve History, https://www.federalreservehistory.org/essays/oil-shock-of-1973–74.

under the twin problems of an oil crisis and droughts, and a third crisis, namely the emergency of 1975, would soon follow. In 1973–75, the government implemented severe monetary and fiscal measures[5] to bring oil prices down and recover from the agricultural supply shock.

When the government looked at industries for restrictions, they turned to Champakbhai for paints. 'Champakbhai was called by the central government to give his opinion on what would happen to the paints industry if imports were to be banned. Champakbhai reassured the company that the paints industry will find a way out and could manage without imports, at least for the time of the crisis that the country was facing,' Girish Choksey told me.

Opportunities in Crises

There was one direct benefit worth noting for Asian Paints from the turmoil. In 1973, the Foreign Exchange Regulation Act (FERA) was passed which made life very difficult for multinational companies in India—and most of the paints companies were multinational, except Asian Paints.

As Gautam Chikermane writes,[6]

> 'The new law imposed restrictions on foreign equity and the growth and expansion of foreign-owned companies: All foreign companies had to dilute their shareholdings to 40 per cent and needed permission from the RBI (as the regulating agency) to operate if their shareholding was higher. Of the 881 companies that applied to retain their higher share, only 150 were allowed; those who found the terms unacceptable began to wind up: Fifty-four companies applied to exit India by 1977–78 and nine in 1980–81.'

[5] Ashima Goyal, 'History of Monetary Policy in India since Independence,' http://www.igidr.ac.in/pdf/publication/WP-2011-018.pdf

[6] Gautam Chikermane, '70 Policies—Foreign Exchange Regulation Act, 1973', ORF, 7 August 2018, https://www.orfonline.org/expert-speak/43065-70-policies-foreign-exchange-regulation-act-

IBM and Coca-Cola famously exited India then.

Some of Asian Paints' biggest competitors saw meaningful changes in ownership during this time:

- Courtaulds reduced its stake in Shalimar Paints (recall that in 1967, it was Shalimar that Asian Paints displaced to become #1) via a public offering in the early 1970s after which the owners lost[7] interest in the company, eventually selling it to Indian businessmen.
- Berger, Jenson, Nicholson (BJN), a subsidiary of Hoechst UK sold[8] part of its stake in British Paints (later Berger Paints) to UB Group in 1976 and exited the company in 1988. Hoechst had a stake in Jenson & Nicholson (India) as well which they divested later.
- Goodlass Nerolac (now Kansai Nerolac) became part of the Tata Forbes group in 1976.

An Internal Emergency Declared at Asian Paints

While the external competitive environment would eventually get better for Asian Paints, there was an 'internal emergency' that was declared by Champakbhai, as veteran employees and family members recall. This was a period of major turmoil as raw material prices went out of control. In 1974 and 1975, materials consumed shot up to 68 per cent of net sales, compared to 64 per cent during 1969–72.

In his memoir, Pramesh Khanna wrote, 'The aftermath of the 1974 oil crisis was felt deeply in terms of raw materials costs and shortages, particularly of phthalic anhydride, which had to be substituted with iso phthalic acid, which increased

[7] Anand Adhikari, 'Shalimar Paints Has Seen Three Ownership Changes', *Business Today*, 7 July 2011, https://www.businesstoday.in/magazine/cover-story/story/history-of-shalimar-paints-22808-2011-06-23.

[8] Saurabh Mukherjea, *The Unusual Billionaires* (2016).

costs.' While sales grew 8 per cent in value terms, margins fell, and post-tax profits fell 21 per cent in 1975.

V.S. Ram, an alumnus of IIT Madras and IIMC, who joined Asian Paints in 1974 told me, 'The company made a loss in the first half of 1975, which was unprecedented and quite unexpected. Bipin Jhaveri wanted to be sure before reporting it to the chairman, so we spent a few sleepless nights going over the books and rechecking the numbers. When it was all done and the numbers checked and tallied, it became clear that we were staring at a significant loss.' By many accounts, volumes had declined, and it was the price hike which increased sales, thus keeping its revenue growth track record intact. A decline in paint volumes was a rare occurrence for the company even back in 1975. But it was the loss in the first half that came as a rude surprise to Champakbhai and the founders.

By 1975, the Bhandup plant was more than fifteen years old and, as per employees of that era, had become inefficient—something that the management knew about but did not address in time. Production processes were slack and there was excess manpower, some of whom were also claiming overtime even when they worked normal hours. Staff costs were 12 per cent of sales in 1975, higher than past averages of around 10–11 per cent.

Champakbhai's Clarion Call

Champakbhai led the efforts to turn around operations at this time. Veeraraghavan recalls him as saying, 'There is nothing whatsoever wrong with the outside world, we are at fault, so the solution has to come from within.' In some instances, he fired staff on the spot. And, just by being physically present at the Bhandup plant more often, he created a sense of crisis and urgency. He pushed for better efficiencies using the computer and cut through a lot of sloth in operations.

Ram told me, 'CHC became the general manager of every department. A lot of people lost their jobs. But he was able to create a sense of urgency and seriousness, making people work together as a team. During that period, working with CHC was much better because CHC would take decisions on the spot.'

As the oil crisis ebbed and the Indian economy got back on track, Asian Paints' financial performance improved—sales grew 18 per cent, material costs dipped to 62 per cent of sales in 1976 and post-tax profits doubled to Rs 73 lakh. In 1979, for the first time, Asian Paints crossed Rs 1 crore in post-tax profits at a time when its effective tax rate[9] was an astronomical 71 per cent.

The Balance Sheet Withstands the Crisis

To its credit, Asian Paints managed its balance sheet well during the crisis. Ram said,

> 'I was hired for corporate planning and strategy but when I came in, the economy was going through extraordinary strains due to sharp increases in commodity prices, and this eventually saw the government and the RBI implement stringent measures to reduce money supply. Credit was hard to come by and the severe credit squeeze put intense pressure on the already tight working capital situation of the company. Bipin Jhaveri, then the financial controller, would bemoan the fact that bank managers, who at one time lined up at his office offering us loans and credit facilities were now making us sit outside their cabins just to plead our case. We looked at every conceivable alternative such as taking loans from cooperative banks, raising fixed deposits, liquidating old inventory, reducing credit limit from debtors, etc.'

The methods worked and to its credit, Asian Paints reduced its debt-equity ratio to 0.87x in 1975 from 1.23x in 1974.

[9] Tax divided by profit before tax.

Sharing his memories of Champakbhai, Ram told me,

'I first met CHC within the first few months of joining in 1974, which was unusual for a fresh recruit, but then I was at the headquarters and being in finance provided opportunities for meetings. Though one of four equal promoters, CHC was obviously way ahead of [the] others and there was an aura of power around him. Yet, he spoke and was expressive so what he said was never complicated. His piercing eyes kept you alert all through the meeting and you knew you couldn't mess around with facts and arguments. He had an easy smile as well, that put one at ease from time to time. He spoke flawless English and kept himself abreast of things happening around the world—and I was impressed that all of this came without the advantage of a pedigree education.

'Some of my internal notes to my boss Mr Jhaveri would get forwarded to him and I would be called for a discussion. He would patiently go through all the calculations and arguments, ask many questions and show a great deal of interest in concepts like discounted cash flows, the effective cost of capital calculations and the impact of taxation policy on our investments. At these meetings, I would often draw his attention to our true cost of capital and the extent to which extremely high rates of taxation prevalent then were playing havoc with the company's ability to generate adequate cash for funding growth. These interactions also provided me the opportunity to propose many steps to chart ways out of the perennial cash crunch we were facing then.'

Champakbhai as Chairman

An interesting observation from the annual reports post internal emergency is the listing of the board of directors and their designations. The chairman is usually the leader of the company and the highest post on the board. In family-owned businesses, the patriarch or the senior-most leader of the family (if the company is run by one family) occupies the position of chairman.

In 1971 and 1972, Suryakant Dani was chairman and (after the internal emergency) in 1978, Champakbhai was chairman and managing director. Champakbhai's ascension to the role of chairman possibly happened between 1973 and 1977—a period for which I do not have annual reports and hence cannot ascertain in which specific year this happened.

Notwithstanding that, I highlight two points: first, as mentioned in Table 3.1 in Chapter 3, Suryakant Dani's name appears first on the list of partners in the original partnership which indicates his seniority, and second, the original Neptune Trading Agency was Suryakant Dani's idea and the origin of the partnership.

Suryakant Dani and Champaklal Choksey were the same age and the closest of friends so the role of chairman switching from one to the other would have happened in the best of spirits and consensus with all the founding families. It is also important to note that in 1973, Asian Paints became a deemed public company dropping the word 'private' from its name, possibly in preparation for an IPO which would eventually happen in 1982.

A Large Cadre of MBAs by the Late 1970s

After the oil crisis and internal emergency was over, Asian Paints went back to business. By 1978, ten years after it hired its first MBAs from IIMA, Asian Paints was a regular at B-Schools. After placement at Asian Paints, the routine of induction and training in Bombay followed by assignment of roles had become a standard operating procedure.

With no official human resource (HR) function in the 1970s, it was Chari who—among his many roles—initially handled the rookies with ample support from Abraham, Jhaveri and Trivedi. Eventually, the job of HR fell to M.M. Khan who went to the IIMs for recruitment. Just like Champakbhai had given Chari full freedom, the culture was passed down.

Here are some stories from the 1970s narrated to me by Munir M. Khan and Fausto Cardoso—both of whom were introduced to me by Veeraraghavan. The four of us had a memorable lunch in March 2023 in Bengaluru with many experiences being recalled, dipped in ample amounts of nostalgia. Khan and Cardoso's stories are followed by Sanjeev Aga who I met a day earlier in Mumbai. Aga has a distinguished career with stints as MD at Blowplast, CEO at the erstwhile Birla-AT&T-Tata and later, Idea Cellular.

Conversations with Ex-employees

Munir M. Khan (IIMC, Batch of 1971, at Asian Paints from 1971 to 1984): Champakbhai was very free and easy-going with the MBAs and always open to suggestions and new ideas for improvements. We could even disagree with him, and he would listen to our argument as long as we were making sense. All of us had a lot of freedom in our jobs and we enjoyed it. Fortunately, he took that stance so everyone else followed the same culture.

That's why (except for CHC) the boss–subordinate relationship at Asian Paints was very different. If someone came up with a good idea, he would approve it. That's the kind of support we had back then. There was trust and freedom within a set of controls. CHC was also an industry leader. At one of the annual Indian Paints Association meets, I recall a director-owner of a paint company asking CHC (IPA chairman then) for advice on how to create a successful company, and CHC replied, 'You have to decide whether *you* want to do well, or you want *the company* to do well.' And he and the other owners of Asian Paints lived by that.

I took over from Kurien as branch manager of Chennai and went on to become all-India sales manager, then shifted as manager of the Bhandup factory. I left as general manager, personnel and Ankleshwar Plant. For me, it was a risk to jump from sales to a factory (many MBAs preferred staying within sales) but I found it very useful for my development.

We tried to convince MBAs to switch roles, sometimes it worked and sometimes it didn't. I was at the Bhandup plant during the 'internal emergency' of the 1970s. Champakbhai brought down the count of workers at the Bhandup plant significantly despite trade unions, who were very powerful then. It was a tough time and so many people got fired that we'd joke about whose wicket was to fall next. But we came out of it, and we built the next plant at Ankleshwar with the same capacity but with half the worker strength. Champakbhai was willing to invest in automation, and to achieve that, he gave us a free hand.

I left Asian Paints in 1984 and it took me two months to decide to resign because I was so well entrenched in the system. I had got an offer from Sadolin Paints, Oman, and would be based in Muscat. I showed the job offer to Atul Choksey who told me that if he was in my place, he would have taken the offer.

He told me that they (Asian Paints) wanted me to stay so if I ever wanted to return to India, I should let them know. Champakbhai invested in MBAs knowing fully well that MBAs are hard to retain for long, could leave at any time, etc. Despite that, he used to say that it didn't matter if they (MBAs) went to the competition, he wanted to provide manpower to the industry! He was a very growth-driven person, it really didn't matter what was happening in the world, whether floods or drought.

Fausto Cardoso (IIM Ahmedabad, Batch of 1973, at Asian Paints from 1973 to 1977): Champakbhai left an indelible impression on my life. He was very open, accessible, not bureaucratic and not ego-driven. I recall an incident that illustrates this, during one of my first interactions with him back in 1973. After our training, we (freshly recruited MBAs) were given our postings. Most were going to large cities like Hyderabad, Jaipur, Mumbai, etc. and I was sent to Guwahati which was a new branch opened some six months earlier. I didn't even know where Guwahati was!

So, I asked Abraham where it was, and he told me to go to CHC since CHC had a map in his cabin. Without hesitation, I knocked on CHC's door and he readily welcomed me in. I told him that I was being sent to Guwahati and had been told to come and meet him. So CHC showed me Guwahati on the map. I asked him why Guwahati. He just said, 'Young man, we have plans for you.' The way he said it, I believed him and accepted it without any doubt.

Trivedibhai was sent along with me and he introduced me to the dealers. That's when the plan started unfolding. In six months, I was promoted to branch manager. Over the next three years, I became manager of bigger branches—Agra and then Bengaluru.

The company was very pragmatic in its approach. For example, when I was at Guwahati, on finding that the initial product mix dispatched to the newly opened branch was out of sync with the market requirement of the region (which was quite different from most parts of the country), it was not difficult to return a significant quantity of stocks to the factory to improve inventory turnover. That was unheard of. My batchmates (in other companies) could not believe it. But that was the culture; if the facts were right, the company would support you.

In an industry dominated by foreign companies, with a sort of 'bada saheb' attitude in most field managers, Asian Paints stood out for its extremely dealer-centric approach and strong presence in mofussil markets. When visiting the dealers, we were different, willing to sit on their 'gaddis' or paint cans and have tea or lunch and get familiar with them.

My stint with Asian Paints was the biggest formative influence in my career. We were not the best paid among our batchmates from the IIMs but arguably among the most fulfilled, entrusted with significant roles and responsibilities relatively early in our careers, and a well-appreciated lot (at this, Khan nodded in the background telling me that I would hear this from many people).

The company was a good training ground thanks to the trust we enjoyed and the early responsibilities in challenging roles. This and the organizational culture placed it among the most preferred employers, attracting some of the best talent including gold medallists from the IIMs.

Sanjeev Aga (IIMC, Batch of 1973, at Asian Paints from 1973 to 1982): By the mid-1960s, Asian Paints was already a company which had made significant headway in the national market share, albeit with small numbers. The two decades before the mid-1960s is not a period I had direct experience of. By 1973 when I joined, Asian Paints wasn't a glamorous company, but we knew it was #1 and our predecessors from IIMC were doing well.

I spent a lot of time in the branches, starting as assistant branch manager at Secunderabad, branch manager (Guwahati and Secunderabad), group product manager in 1980 and regional sales manager (North and East) in 1981. It was about the best company I could have joined, though I say this only in retrospect. My years as branch manager of the Guwahati branch were formative as it was my first leadership stint. We were learning but were not aware of how much we were learning. None of us at that time thought that we were part of building an exceptional company in our sector, and generally in the Indian industry. When a company outperforms in a competitive environment, it is the hundred small things it does incrementally better and a culture that can absorb change and promote further change that propels it.

I think that the key driver was that Asian Paints assembled a large number of young, educated people (all under thirty) from across Indian geographies, most of whom started in field sales, some in finance and IT, but soon spread to manufacturing and supply chain. Incidentally, terms like IT and supply chain did not even exist then. Many companies (even multi-national companies) could not implement new ideas because they did not have a critical mass of receptive people to implement. A less-known factor was that Asian Paints had people to whom it would never even occur to make a dishonest buck. That removed a constraint that impeded most companies from putting ideas into practice with rapidity and fidelity. So that's the first thing.

The second thing: if you want to implement, say RPPD, or the earliest forecast-linked production planning and distribution scheme in 1975 . . . the idea may originate from anyone, but there were equally bright people across India to effortlessly absorb and execute those ideas—you just had to send a circular and your idea would be executed. Such improvements did not usually arise in the competition, because they were change-averse, but even if they wanted to, the wider organization resisted change or would not grasp the import of the change. This may be an uncharitable over-generalization. But Asian Paints could do things differently because they had young, educated people with a predisposition for doing things differently and better.

My interactions with CHC were not that many, since I was mainly in the branches, and he'd also had his heart attack and was taking a back seat. So, a lot of my views on CHC are inferences and insights, some of which dawned on me only after I left Asian Paints. He grew in my estimation after I left Asian Paints. Sometimes, time provides perspective. In summary, I'd say he was like a diamond in the rough. He was not a rounded manager, but the rough edges did not harm him as he delegated management to others. He did not have a classical education, but he had a presence and exuded a strong personality. And he thought much harder and much deeper than anyone else, deeper than most other people I have known. And his observations were equally deep and first-hand. No one is completely original, but CHC was substantively original.

Think of it. Which other Indian promoter would take a boy in his early twenties, whom he does not know, who he has never met before, and yet be completely comfortable sending him to, say, head a branch in Cochin, with very little oversight?

CHC intuitively grasped that personal character, and the power of the human mind, are the two most important competitive advantages. A lot of good stuff at Asian Paints can be traced to these two building blocks.

Part 4

Spreading Wings

Chapter 9

Expansions and Diversifications

'Never allow a good crisis go to waste. It's an opportunity to do the things you once thought were impossible.'

—Rahm Emanuel, Chief of Staff to US President Barack Obama[1]

Asian Paints learnt a lot from its own crisis and emerged stronger from the internal emergency of 1975. With a large cadre of MBAs in place, and the second generation learning to lead the charge, the time was ripe to expand. And, Asian Paints grew aggressively in the 1980s.

First came the expansion within the core business (three manufacturing plants—Ankleshwar, Patancheru, Kasna—were commissioned from 1981 to 1990), across related products (vinyl pyridine latex), and backward integration (phthalic anhydride and pentaerythritol); second were the overseas launches (South Pacific) and foreign collaborations (Devoe Martin, Nippon, Sigma, PPG). This chapter focuses on the expansion within India, and the next chapter looks at overseas expansions and technical collaborations.

[1] Rahm Emanuel, 'Let's Make Sure this Crisis Doesn't Go to Waste', *Washington Post*, 25 March 2020, https://www.washingtonpost.com/opinions/2020/03/25/lets-make-sure-this-crisis-doesnt-go-waste/.

The 1980s—A Big Leap Forward

To truly understand Asian Paints' scale of growth in the 1980s, one needs to compare it to its rivals, and this is how the comparison looked (Table 9.1 below). In 1977, Asian Paints was 1.4x the second player, by 1987, the gap increased to 1.9x, and this excludes the likes of Shalimar Paints, Jenson & Nicholson and Garware Paints, all of whom would drop out of the top players list. Recall that by the 1970s and the 1980s, the market was shifting towards decorative, away from industrial, and household paints was the battleground. Despite the highly competitive intensity, Asian Paints was able to increase its market share, making its achievement even more notable.

Table 9.1: Asian Paints versus competition in the paints industry

Net sales (Rs in crore)	1977	1987
Asian Paints	23.2	155.2
Kansai Nerolac (then Goodlass Nerolac)	17.2	80.1
Berger Paints (then British Paints)	11.8	60.6

(Source: Annual reports. Note: 1) the comparison is based on the top three players in 1987; 2) net sales are gross sales minus excise duty, rebates, discounts, etc. as stated in annual reports.)

Let us now look at the expansion within India in three sections—expansion of manufacturing facilities, diversification into related products and backward integration.

Section 1: Expansion of Manufacturing Facilities

Among the many lessons learnt were improving product quality and technical capabilities (for which a computer-aided colour system was installed in Bhandup in 1979) and strengthening management depth (for which hiring MBAs was now a routine affair). The transition to the next generation was also underway.

In the 1980 chairman's letter, Champakbhai specifically mentioned 'organizational restructuring' as an attempt to realize 'the potential presented by people'. One member each from the four families was well entrenched within the company across departments and divisions before eventually getting elevated to the board. The board of directors in the 1980 annual report included Ashwin Dani, Ashwin Choksi and Atul Choksey as full-time directors, and Abhay Vakil joined the board in 1983.

Strong Line of Managerial Talent

Strengthening the depth of the second generation of founders in 1978 were the next line of non-family leaders (or managers, which was then the highest designation), which included Chari (administration and general management), C.V. Abraham (marketing), C.J. Bhumkar (technical), Bipinbhai Jhaveri (financial controller), M.M. Khan (factory), Ajit Mantagani (sales), B.R. Trivedi (exports), V. Veeraraghavan (systems), etc. and various heads of branch sales and divisional sales. In a decade, Asian Paints had transformed into a market leader with depth and width in resources and a young cadre of professionals across India. Expansion, therefore, became easier.

Expanding in the Licence Raj

Externally, however, expansion depended on the governments in charge. This was, after all, the era of the licence raj. The Industries (Development and Regulation) Act, 1951 was in place. The law declared 'in public interest' that the central government 'should take under its control' the industries specified in the First Schedule.[2] Paints were included[3] under Section C, clause 19 (5) of the First Schedule and hence fell squarely under central government purview.

---

[2] Gautam Chikermane, *70 Policies that Shaped India*, Observer Research Foundation, 2018.

[3] https://eaindustry.nic.in/pdf_files/IndustriesAct_1951.pdf, accessed on 6 January 2023.

Opening a new plant and adding fresh capacity meant applying for and waiting to be granted a licence. This long-winded procedure involved dealing with the central government and, typically, whoever was the minister of industries. The licence raj was not the only hurdle that Asian Paints successfully crossed during its expansion phase in the 1980s. There was also the rise of militant trade unions in India.

Labour Problems at Bhandup

As Professor Roy writes,[4] the 1970s and the early 1980s witnessed a spate of violent strikes in the older industries, especially cotton textiles, jute textiles and engineering. In January 1982, the Bombay cotton mill workers went on a strike that officially lasted eighteen months and involved more than 2,00,000 workers. Roy adds further that organized unions in Bombay were political actors, and preferred negotiations to strike.

In 1981, the Bhandup plant witnessed two disruptions caused by labour problems as well as two fires, one which affected the production of resins for a month and another that gutted their R&D lab. Fortunately, sales and revenues in 1981 were not affected by these disruptions. In 1983, a comprehensive agreement valid for three years was signed between the company and the workers at the Bhandup plant. While staff costs as a percentage of sales rose to 8.9 per cent of net sales in 1983 (8.2 per cent in 1982) as a result of the agreement, a sizeable improvement in productivity was also agreed upon as part of the settlement.

However, rivalry between trade unions was[5] common in Bombay in the 1980s. Unfortunately for Asian Paints, one such

[4] Tirthankar Roy, *A History of Business in India.*

[5] Smruti Koppikar, 'Datta Samant's Killing Puts Focus on New Breed of Labour Leaders with "Broker" Status', *India Today*, 17 April 2013, https://www.indiatoday.in/magazine/states/story/19970215-datta-samant-killing-puts-focus-on-new-breed-of-labour-leaders-with-broker-status-832845-1997-02-14.

fight between the officially recognized trade union and another rival union resulted in a long-drawn-out partial strike that lasted almost six months. While the company weathered the storm well, net revenue growth of just 8 per cent in 1986 was the lowest since the internal emergency year of 1975.

Bhandup paint production quantity fell 43 per cent but thanks to higher production at Ankleshwar and a sharp jump at Patancheru, the company was able to show an overall revenue growth.

Berger Paints (then British Paints) also had a lockout in Kolkata back in 1979 which lasted for seven and a half months, due to which the company reported a loss in both 1979 and 1980. The strike was so severe that the management took the extreme step of approaching competitors (including Asian Paints) to manufacture for them.

As the 1979 directors' report states, 'Your Company, therefore, undertook processing of its goods at outside paint manufacturing units located in various parts of the country under the supervision of and technical and quality control by its own officials. But for this measure, the loss suffered by the Company would have been higher.'

Apart from the 1986 lockout at Bhandup, labour relations at Asian Paints remained generally cordial through the 1980s and the 1990s, and Asian Paints signed productivity-linked agreements with their workers at all three factories (including Taloja for VPL) at regular intervals. There was yet another major fire at the Bhandup plant in 1996 with losses to materials stored, but no major loss to the manufacturing units and R&D labs.

Going back to the 1980s, three manufacturing facilities were added after the internal emergency. Manufacturing facilities in 'notified backward areas' would get benefits from the government which would improve overall capital efficiencies. Setting up plants in collaboration with SIDCs (state industrial development corporations like GIDC for Gujarat and UPSIDC for Uttar Pradesh) ensured that major factors like land allocation, acquisition and signing of leases were smooth. Added to this, widening the geographical spread would help the company expand across India.

Here is an overview of the three new plants.

1. Ankleshwar, Gujarat—1981

Ankleshwar is a city in the Bharuch district of Gujarat, located just under 350 km from Mumbai, with Surat to its south and Baroda to its north, and hence well connected to larger cities within Gujarat. With the Bhandup plant capacity nearing its peak, the founders were looking for a new area to set up their next plant. The founders were familiar with Gujarat and chose Ankleshwar as a base to set up their new factory.

The new factory would drive two major expansions—first a new product in the form of auto finishes, and then fresh capacity to augment Bhandup. In 1978, Asian Paints successfully introduced Krilo which was an acrylic automotive finish aimed at the automotive industry. India's car industry at that time[6] had only three major players—Hindustan Motors in Kolkata (Ambassador car), Premier Automobiles in Mumbai (Premier Padmini) and Standard Motor Products in Chennai (Standard Herald). However, plans were afoot to make a people's car which eventually became Maruti Udyog Limited in 1981. Thus, a calculated entry into the automotive industry made sense for the founders back in the 1970s.

Land acquisition, construction and financing of the automotive finish and refinish facilities at Ankleshwar happened from 1978 to 1980. State Bank of India (SBI) and Gujarat Industrial Investment Corporation sanctioned Rs 75 lakh in aggregate towards the project, in addition to which Asian Paints was also eligible for central and state cash subsidies.

[6] R.C. Bhargava and Seetha, *The Maruti Story: How a Public Sector Company Put India on Wheels* Collins, 2010.

In the licence raj era of the late 1970s, Asian Paints applied for and received an industrial licence for substantial expansion of its capacity. The government approved a fresh capacity of 15,000 MT at Ankleshwar which was commissioned on 1 April 1981. To put things in perspective, in the same financial year (1980), Asian Paint sold 21,879 tonnes of paints and enamels from the Bhandup plant.

The plant at Ankleshwar was also much more modern than Bhandup, as Champakbhai and the founders had learnt their lessons from the internal emergency. The second generation of founders, along with Chari, spent a lot of time planning the manufacturing facilities right till the commissioning.

Champakbhai's philosophy of having a 'champion' for each project was also shaping up—in the case of Ankleshwar, Khan was elevated to general manager for the plant in 1981, one of his last assignments before he left and would be replaced by P. Ananthanarayanan. The Ankleshwar plant would significantly augment Asian Paints' capacities and efficiencies, as well as entry into products such as automotive finishes. Asian Paints kept expanding in Ankleshwar, acquiring 15 acres in 1986 for manufacturing phthalic anhydride as part of its backward integration plans.

2. Patancheru, Telangana—1985

Even as the first phase of expansion at Ankleshwar was rolling out, Asian Paints began planning for another location for its next plant which would be outside western India. This time, they chose the south. In 1982, the organization got the approvals for 15,000 MT capacity and acquired land in Patancheru which was then in Andhra Pradesh (today in Telangana) and around 35 km from Hyderabad. ICICI Bank and SBI sanctioned[7] term loans of Rs 1.75 crore for the project. Like Ankleshwar, the

[7] 1984 annual report.

Patancheru plant was commissioned in phases with Phase 1 in 1985 and Phase 2 in 1986.

J.N. Shahani who was then heading the Engineering Services function was tasked with setting up the Patancheru plant, and V.S. Ram was appointed as the first factory head. I met Ram in Mumbai, and he shared his recollections from his long tenure at Asian Paints. Ram worked with Jhaveri in finance, and the two set about navigating the company, first through the 1975 internal emergency, meeting its working capital challenges, and then gradually making the transformation from a cash short to a cash surplus entity and from a closely held to a listed public company. In 1985, after a decade in finance, he moved as the manager of the Patancheru factory.

Ram spent thirty-four years in Asian Paints across various roles before leaving in 2008. Asian Paints also has an emotional connection to Ram since it was Chari who provided a good reference when Ram's future father-in-law inquired about Ram for an alliance with his daughter. A few years after retirement, at the request of Biji Kurien and the Indian Paint Association, Ram set up the Paints & Skilling Council, a not-for-profit company for skill development in the paints and coatings industry.

Ram said,

> 'Labour productivity was very important back then in Asian Paints. Initially, many managers tended to see productivity in purely cost-benefit terms [with the investments having to be justified by the savings from the productivity improvements they brought in], but Choksey had a different take on the subject. In his view, any productivity improvement was worth pursuing, even if the cost was somewhat higher than justified. To him, the visible cost of a large workforce was only a part of the story: the invisible costs were much higher and merited an aggressive trade-off. Strident trade unionism of the late seventies and eighties helped to strengthen this resolve and resulted in manpower productivity becoming a key metric at all levels at the plants. This is also the period when, first

proposed by M.M. Khan, productivity negotiation and documentation became a feature of every wage settlement between unions and the company.

'The Ankleshwar plant, once production stabilized, was twice as productive as the Bhandup plant. This opened the eyes of managers to the enormous improvement that was possible in a new facility unfettered by the entrenched restrictive practices rife in an older facility. The fact that there were quality issues arising from the faster pace of work at Ankleshwar did not dampen the enthusiasm for capturing and locking in the improved output norms.

'When Patancheru was being commissioned, expectations ran high. On the one hand, a further improvement in productivity compared to Ankleshwar was seen as a 'given'. On the other hand, there were also voices of caution advocating that a slight sacrifice on productivity vis-à-vis Ankleshwar but addressing all the quality concerns would be the way to go.

It is in this background that the team at Patancheru set about the task of starting up the plant. The time that the team had before commissioning was put to good use, analysing every production job in great detail, looking at alternate ways of doing things, studying the experiences of others, especially Japanese practices, and arriving at a shared understanding that productivity and quality were not mutually opposing aims. There was a general consensus that the plant should focus on improved work design and better practices to achieve both high productivity and meet quality standards.

'Once the team was sold on this philosophy, progress was easy. Some [team members] were MBAs, some came from Bhandup, and some with experience from other factories. Our approach was never to speak about productivity explicitly but to work on quality and good plant practices, the belief being that if these were taken care of, productivity would follow. I even secured a promise from Atul Choksey—that for one year he would not ask me about productivity or raise the subject in his meetings with plant managers (although I knew that he secretly asked Murty how we were doing, from time to time).

'We did things differently. For example, our job listing was what each worker would do, not what each group or clique of workers would do. Employees participated in deciding how tasks would be performed, they were not just directed from above. People were encouraged to come up with small innovations and new ideas, and the engineering wing of the plant was adequately funded to do numerous trials of new ideas. The plant demonstrated that we could achieve very high productivity with the then-existing technology while ensuring quality and good practices. Many of the innovations and changes at the plant—such as small work teams, self-supervised worker groups, devolution of greater responsibility to operators, formal protocols for effluent treatment, reuse of [effluent waters] and deployment of engineers on the shop floor—were found to work well and were to varying degrees replicated at the other locations.

'So, in many ways, I saw the Patancheru [factory] as a laboratory where we were trying to do things differently and the entire company was enthusiastically cheering us and providing support.'

3. Kasna, Uttar Pradesh—1990

In 1986, after the commissioning of Phase 2 of Patancheru, Asian Paints got a letter of intent from the government for 23,000 MT of new capacity to be installed in the state of Uttar Pradesh (UP). Ram was given the additional responsibility for engineering services to finalize the location and establish the factory.

Ram and his engineering team toured various locations in UP like Kanpur, Dehat, Etawah, Unnao, Bulandshahar, Bareilly and Barabanki before settling on Kasna which comes under the Greater Noida area in the National Capital Region (NCR), about 25 km from Delhi. Land was leased from the UP State Industrial Corporation in 1986 and the plant, with a capacity of 16,000 MT in the first phase, was commissioned in March 1990. SBI sanctioned[8] financial assistance of Rs 7 crore towards part financing of the first phase.

> 'Though located just 11 km from the Surajpur industrial estate, Kasna was totally undeveloped, notorious for dacoity and violence between opposing gangs. But when we saw the NCR plan, we knew it would eventually turn out to be a nice location, well connected in future. Initially, we faced a lot of challenges. People weren't willing to work there, especially white-collar staff—you couldn't walk the streets at night. Many of our staff quit, personnel turnover was high, it was difficult to hire good graduate chemists and engineers, and the local mafia would threaten employees. Kasna was our most challenging plant,' Ram told me.

Many ex-employees mentioned that at various points in time, Champakbhai and Atul Choksey considered shutting down Kasna. It was only on the insistence of employees like Ram that they persisted. Ram was called back to Bombay in 1991/92 after circulating between Patancheru, Kasna and engineering services. And the man who took over from Ram was K.B.S. Anand.

K.B.S. Anand has already been introduced and quoted in previous chapters and hence needs no introduction. An IIT Bombay (1978) and IIM Calcutta (1979) alumnus, Anand spent more than forty years at Asian Paints leaving as the MD and CEO in 2020. After joining Asian Paints in 1979, Anand was posted in Jaipur and was shifted temporarily to Bombay when his father passed away.

After spending almost a decade in various roles, Anand was frustrated and went to Chari who promoted him to factory

---

[8] 1990 annual report.

manager at Kasna and, later to general manager of both the Kasna and Patancheru plants. It was Anand who would go on to lead and streamline the Kasna plant and not without challenges.

'I was a regular Bombay guy, to be honest. I grew up in Bombay and my initial education was in Bombay. I used to believe that Hindi movies are the greatest exaggeration in the world. I went to UP and realized Hindi movies don't even tell you 50 per cent of life,' he told me with a wry smile.

He added,

> 'The workforce was local and—like other companies did in that era—hiring was done via local goondas. I've seen the worst side of cops, politicians and goondas. At one point of time, I had an armed guard and my son was thrilled to see that. But we overcame all the challenges and established the factory, getting production, recruitment and management in place over time. In the end, all of us, including the goondas, became friends and I never paid a paisa in my life there at that time.'

Section 2: Diversification into Related Products

The diversification needs some context because the planning for these products was before the internal emergency of 1975. As the second generation was growing up, Champakbhai and the founders decided to enter new products which would be related to paints but housed either outside of Asian Paints or as divisions.

This would serve three purposes—to ensure that the second generation (of which there was a sizeable pool) had their own businesses, that these products could also be sold to Asian Paints, and that any excess capacity could be sold in the open market. Obviously, in today's context, promoter-held private businesses with linkages to the listed entity are not the best form of corporate governance; but let's remember that Asian Paints was a private company in the 1970s.

Diversifications into Synthetic Resins and VPL

The first diversification was synthetic resins and the second was vinyl pyridine latex (VPL). Both were ideal candidates for import substitutions which was a rising trend in the 1970s. Synthetic resins were housed in a private limited company, Resins and Plastics Limited (RPL). VPL started as a division within Asian Paints and was later hived off into Apcotex Lattices (ALL). At various points of time, all four families held stakes in both companies; subsequently, these stakes would be unwound and separated so that today, the Chokseys head Apcotex and the remaining three families head RPL. First, we discuss RPL and then ALL.

1. RPL is a manufacturer of synthetic resins. RPL was initially promoted by all four founders of Asian Paints, including the Chokseys. Currently, RPL's promoters are the Choksis, Danis and Vakils, the present promoters of Asian Paints. As per its website, RPL started operations in 1971 to manufacture a variety of resins such as alkyd resins, acrylic resins, epoxy resins, ketonic resins, maleic resins, melamine formaldehyde resins, organic compounds, polyester resins, polymide resins, phenolic resins and urea-formaldehyde resins, some of which are import substitutes. RPL, which is currently not listed on the stock exchanges, has manufacturing facilities in Taloja and Ankleshwar and its FY23 total income stood at Rs 253.2 crore with profit at tax at Rs 9.8 crore.
2. For the purposes of this book, the second company, Apcotex Industries, needs a longer discussion since it is currently the flagship company of Atul Choksey. Land for the VPL project (and other projects) was taken in the Taloja industrial area, around 40 km from Mumbai in the Navi Mumbai satellite township. The VPL plant was constructed in 1979, for which Asian Paints availed

> term loans of Rs 55 lakh, just over 10 per cent of the total debt of Rs 5 crore on the 1979 balance sheet.

Davy Power Gas (which later became part of Aker Kvaerner group) was the consultant for the project. S Rengachari, an MSc (Tech) and PhD who joined Asian Paints in 1977 as a technical executive (projects) was later appointed as manager of the Apcotex division. Technology was purchased on a lump sum and royalty basis from German chemical major Chemische Werke Hüls which became[9] part of Evonik. In 1987, manufacturing facilities for synthetic rubber lattices (SRL) were commissioned with a capacity of 1200 MT.

Apcotex—Carved Out in 1991

In 1989, Apcotex Lattices Limited (ALL) was a 100 per cent subsidiary of Asian Paints, and in 1991, it was carved out of Asian Paints into a separate company. The scheme of arrangement was approved by all relevant authorities, including the Bombay High Court, the central government, as well as shareholders. Shares in ALL were allotted to Asian Paints shareholders.

How large was Apcotex when it was carved out of Asian Paints? Since it was formed, Apcotex sales rose steadily (barring 1983) reaching Rs 10 crore in 1991, or 3 per cent of Asian Paints' gross sales. Profits were Rs 95.77 lakh, around 6 per cent of Asian Paints' total post-tax profits. Thus, Apcotex was relatively small, and given that the founders were already focusing on many other things, they possibly decided to carve out the division to let it grow separately.

Why is Apcotex important? Because this was the company that Atul Choksey would go on to lead after the Chokseys split with Asian Paints in 1997. After the split, Apcotex did an IPO in 1997 with a unique feature of reservation of up to 50 per cent

[9] 'History of Hüls AG - Evonik Industries', 28 July 2020, https://history.evonik.com/en/predecessor-companies/huels.

(of the total IPO size) for its existing small odd-lot shareholders (from the earlier issue of shares to Asian Paints), providing them an opportunity to convert their odd-lot shareholdings into a marketable lot.[10]

Today, Apcotex specializes in emulsion polymer products and is among India's leading producers of synthetic rubber (NBR & HSR) and synthetic latex (nitrile, VP latex, XSB & Acrylic latex) based on styrene-butadiene chemistry and butadiene-acrylonitrile chemistry. Apcotex is currently majority held by Atul Choksey who is the chairman of the company, while Atul's son Abhiraj is the managing director. Apcotex FY23 revenues stood at Rs 1080 crore with profit after tax of Rs 108 crore.

Section 3: Backward Integration

'Make or buy' is a typical business decision that promoters face in situations where they consider manufacturing a product in-house or simply purchasing it from the market and selling it. Each option has its pay-offs, and the decision of making or buying depends on many factors such as financial strength, marketing capabilities, etc.

In the FMCG industry, for example, companies may hire contracted manufacturers to make the product so that they can simply focus on their own strengths—namely distributing goods across India and marketing their brand. Bharti Airtel's famous 'minutes factory model' in the 2000s successfully used outside vendors for many activities while focusing on selling the 'Airtel' brand.

Reliance Industries (RIL), on the other hand, is possibly the biggest example in India of a company going from manufacturing the finished products to manufacturing the raw materials as well. For example, it started with selling textiles

[10] A 'lot' meant a rounded-up minimum quantity of shares (like 5, 10, 50, 100, etc.) that could be traded on the stock exchange, in the pre-electronic era of the stock market.

and eventually went all the way to petrochemicals, refining and exploration. This 'moving back' or 'moving up' is known as backward integration. There is no clear verdict[11] on which choice is the best between make or buy; what a company chooses will depend on many factors.

In the 1980s, Asian Paints decided to manufacture two key raw materials—pentaerythritol and phthalic anhydride—on its own, instead of buying them from suppliers. While the first was a joint venture, the second was made completely in-house.

1. Pentaerythritol, Pentasia Chemicals (1984)

Pentaerythritol is a chemical with a wide variety of uses from plastics and paints to cosmetics and explosives. In 1984, Asian Paints signed a joint venture agreement with Tamil Nadu Industrial Development Corporation (TIDCO) to establish a joint venture company to manufacture 3000 MT of pentaerythritol and 1800 MT of sodium formate (used in the chemical industry). The company was called Pentasia Chemicals Limited (PCL), and the plant was located at Cuddalore which was a centrally notified backward area.

PCL did an IPO in August 1986 which was oversubscribed thirty-eight times. The plant was commissioned in March 1987, with William Smith of Hercules Inc. (a technical collaborator in the project, now part of Ashland Inc.) switching on the reactor at the Cuddalore plant.

Unfortunately, the venture went from one misfortune to another, starting with initial teething problems and methane shortage in 1987 to a labour strike in 1991 and a lockout from August 1992 to April 1993.

Asian Paints bought TIDCO's stake in the company in 1991, coincidentally the same year as the separation of the Apcotex division. By 1994, accumulated losses stood at Rs 10.9 crore

[11] Robert D. Buzzell, 'Is Vertical Integration Profitable?', *Harvard Business Review*, 1 August 2014, https://hbr.org/1983/01/is-vertical-integration-profitable.

(versus the book value of Asian Paints investment which stood at Rs 6.8 crore) and the company went to the Board for Industrial and Financial Reconstruction (BIFR), the earlier version of the bankruptcy system. In 1996, as part of a scheme sanctioned by the BIFR, PCL was merged with Asian Paints.

2. Phthalic Anhydride, Ankleshwar Factory (1987)

In 1986, Asian Paints acquired 15 acres of land in GIDC Industrial Estate, Ankleshwar and applied to the government for a licence to build a 15,000-MT plant to manufacture phthalic anhydride. SBI part-financed the project to the extent of Rs 10 crore. The plant was commissioned in March 1990, and in 1991, during the Gulf Crisis, was useful to keep raw material costs in moderation. 'First, we set up a resin and paints plant at Ankleshwar and then we made our phthalic anhydride. J.N. Shahani from engineering services and I went to Germany for this purpose,' Atul Choksey told me. The plant was made with 'Von Heyden' low-energy process technology provided by Wacker Chemie through Davy McKee AG, Germany.

Both the divisions went on to do well for Asian Paints, reporting sales of Rs 100 crore (Rs 75 crore for phthalic anhydride and Rs 25 crore for pentaerythritol and sodium formate) in FY1997 which amounted to more than 10 per cent of that year's gross sales of Rs 937.6 crore.

A Temporary Foray into Pesticides

Before we move to the next chapter, a passing mention must be made of a diversification that did not last very long. The 1978 annual report mentions one new project—pesticides under a 100 per cent subsidiary called Ankur Chemicals. 'We planned to manufacture fungicides based on MBC [Carbendazim] and had tied up with Regional Research Laboratory, Hyderabad. BASF sells this under the Bavistin brand. Soon, we realized that this was not for us and wound up the venture before much progress or investment had been made,' Atul Choksey told me.

In the next chapter, we explore Asian Paints' diversifications overseas as well as its technical collaborations to enter new segments.

Chapter 10

Collaborations and Foreign Forays

'If you want to go fast, go alone. If you want to go far, go together.'

—African proverb

In the previous chapter, we looked at expansion within India in terms of new plants, diversification and backward integration. In this chapter we look at Asian Paints' journey outside India,[1] its technical collaborations with foreign partners, its IPO in 1982 and the transition to the next generation.

Section 1: Asian Paints' Overseas Expansions

Asian Paints was exporting paints early on but in a limited way. The 1971 annual report shows exports of Rs 36.35 lakh from gross sales of Rs 9.4 crore, or less than 5 per cent. By 1978, this had grown to Rs 1 crore in gross sales of Rs 34.6 crore, still less than 5 per cent. Champakbhai and the founders had an eye on global markets but were probably unsure of making a large bet, given that they already had expansion plans within India. And therefore, to be on the safe side, just like the first IIM and the

[1] The story of Asian Paints expansion in the South Pacific and Australia is based on the memoirs of P.N. Khanna.

first state to expand were both in Gujarat, they chose a country with a sizeable Indian Gujarati population.

The Gujarati community has a long and rich history[2] in the Fiji Islands, an archipelago of islands in the South Pacific Ocean. Asian Paints became the first Indian paints company to set up a subsidiary abroad, which was its factory in the Fiji Islands in 1978. This footprint would be expanded from Fiji to cover the Tonga Islands, Solomon Islands, Vanuatu and Queensland (Australia).

The man to lead this was P.N. Khanna, who had joined Asian Paints in 1962 as a young engineer from HBT University Kanpur. 'Khanna is an honest, straightforward man with strong ethics and integrity. He laid the foundation for the overseas business,' Atul Choksey told me. Recalling his early memories, Khanna, now eighty-five years old, told me, 'Champakbhai was a father figure to us. Dr Kudva had left Asian Paints in 1967 and Champakbhai kept encouraging us to keep working hard.'

Asian Paints was exporting to Fiji but the time taken to reach the islands from the Bhandup factory ran into months. Purushottam Kalidas Kasabia, the agent selling the paints in Fiji, reached out to Champakbhai and the founders to discuss the idea of setting up the plant. V.S. Ram recalled, with some amusement, of the time he was told to make a project report for the Fiji venture, to be distributed to government agencies and potential lenders and bankers.

> 'Chari called me and said, "I am going to Fiji, so please prepare a project report." We knew nothing about the market, had no data other than what Mr Kasabia bought from us and little by way of other commercial information, local rules and laws, etc. Time was short and with hardly any authentic information to go by, we prepared a project report using information gathered

[2] Wikipedia contributors, 'Gujaratis in Fiji', Wikipedia, 29 January 2022, https://en.wikipedia.org/w/index.php?title=Gujaratis_in_Fiji&oldid=1068682533, last revised on 22 January 2022, last accessed on 6 June 2023.

from travel brochures and the size of neighbouring markets like Australia! My great surprise was when Mr Chari returned from the tour and said that the report was very well received!'

Chari, Khanna and Trivedi made exploratory visits and discovered that a) there was competition from both global brands like Berger and ICI as well as Australian and New Zealand paints companies like Taubmans Paints (which Asian Paints would acquire[3] in 2003) and Resene Paints present in Fiji; b) the product range in Fiji was very different from that in India; and c) raw materials would have to be imported from neighbouring Australia and New Zealand. But the most unique feature of the Fiji Islands was that dealers used tinting machines which were yet to be introduced in India. This is where Asian Paints decided to make the company a joint venture, offering equity to dealers.

Thus, Asian Paints (South Pacific) was incorporated as a 51 per cent joint venture with the remaining 49 per cent being held by a variety of dealers and agents, including Purushottam Kasabia and another Fiji local, Vinod Shankarbhai Patel, both of whom, along with Pramesh Khanna, would be on the board of the company. The plant commenced commercial production in 1978 at Lautoka, a large city and the sugar cane growing district in Viti Levu, the largest island of Fiji.

Recalling the time he left India, Khanna recollected in his memoirs, 'Just before leaving for Fiji, I went to see Mr C.H. Choksey. He simply asked what the investment was in the project. I said, "Rs 10 lakh." He told me not to worry about the money, just that he wanted us to create a name for Asian Paints overseas.' Chari was more circumspect, warning Khanna that if the venture failed, it would be difficult for him to readjust back to the parent company which would have moved on significantly. It was thus, sink or swim.

---

[3] Baiju Kalesh, 'Asian Paints Acquires Fiji Company', *Times of India*, 11 September 2003, https://timesofindia.indiatimes.com/business/india-business/asian-paints-acquires-fiji-company/articleshow/177292.cms.

And Khanna swam with elan. He would go on to spend twenty-six years abroad for Asian Paints, in his forty-two-year career (1962 to 2004). In his time, the retirement age for executives was fifty-five years but for Khanna, this was extended to sixty-five years.

The initial days were tough but the partnership with Kasabia and Patel eased the adjustment for the Khannas in a foreign land. In 1979, Asian Paints sent over Amitav Sur and Subhash Sehgal to strengthen the team. All three—Khanna, Sur and Sehgal—would join the board of Asian Paints (South Pacific) in 1981.

The dealers accommodated Asian Paints among the foreign brands since they were effectively owner-distributors given their equity shareholding in the venture. The company made a marginal profit in the first year of operations. The company also survived many hurricanes and storms (which also became opportunities for home reconstruction) and even a military coup in 1987 to eventually become the largest paints company in the Fiji Islands.

Asian Paints began exports from Fiji, and Khanna led many export delegations to neighbouring countries which resulted in the company expanding to Tonga and the Solomon Islands in the 1980s and Vanuatu and Australia in the 1990s. Asian Paints had already expanded to Nepal in 1984.

Over time, the South Pacific would become a small percentage of Asian Paints' international revenues as it expanded across the globe, setting up operations as well as making acquisitions; in November 2002 it acquired[4] a 50 per cent stake in Berger International Singapore (which Pramesh Khanna would lead as CEO) and a 60 per cent stake in SCIB Chemical SAE Egypt. It also exited[5] some countries such as Hong Kong, Malaysia,

[4] Times News Network, 'Asian Paints Takes 50 Pc in Berger', *Times of India*, 5 September 2002, https://timesofindia.indiatimes.com/business/india-business/asian-paints-takes-50-pc-in-berger/articleshow/21297928.cms.

[5] Reuters Staff, 'Asian Paints to Exit from Thailand, China by End-Feb', Reuters, 25 January 2010, https://www.reuters.com/article/asian-paints-operations-idINBMB00957520100125.

Thailand and China in 2010. The 2023 annual report provides the following latest breakdown of international revenues:

Table 10.1: Asian Paints international revenues (percentage)

Region	Countries	Percentage of international revenues
Asia	Bangladesh, Nepal, Sri Lanka, Indonesia	44.4
Middle East	Oman, Bahrain, UAE and Qatar	29.2
Africa	Egypt and Ethiopia	22.0
South Pacific	Fiji, Solomon Islands, Samoa and Vanuatu	4.4

(Source: 2023 annual report, page 16)

Khanna went from chief executive of Asian Paints South Pacific to director South Pacific region and finally retired in 2004. Acknowledging the contributions of Asian Paints in his memoirs, he specifically thanked Chari ('who had been an excellent boss, friend, philosopher & guide throughout my career with Asian Paints') and praised 'the support, inspiration and guidance provided by the directors—Mr Choksey, Mr Madhukar and Mr Chari at every stage was immense and unforgettable'.

From Core Competence to Distinctive Competence

Jagdish Acharya worked with Khanna in Fiji before becoming chief executive at the Vanuatu operation when it started in 1992. Acharya is a gold medallist from the IIMC batch of 1979 and spent thirty-five years at Asian Paints. We met in Mumbai, and he told me, 'From 1979 to 1985, I worked in the branches starting with Agra, then going to Patna and Calcutta. In 1985, they [Asian Paints] asked me to go to Fiji but on the condition that I get married! I think CHC had it in mind, but it was Chari who told me. It was a thoughtful idea. Of course, I got married and we left as a newly married couple for Fiji.'

Acharya testified to the major strengths of Asian Paints, discussed earlier in the books, namely kitchen relationships with dealers, a vibrant working environment largely free from politics, Champakbhai's encouragement and trust in young MBAs, and taking very good care of their employees.

Whenever Acharya visited India, Chari would take him to Champakbhai who would first ask him about his family before asking about business. And this concern went back to the time when Acharya was to leave for Fiji. 'Abraham came to meet my father [who had had a heart attack sometime earlier] to tell him, "Your son is going to Fiji; we hope that is fine with you." So that kind of concern was always a big positive for me,' Acharya told me.

Acharya spoke of how Asian Paints went from building competence to refining it to a core competence and then making it a distinctive competence. He spoke of how the distribution system moved from the branches telling the factory what to produce and distribute to the computer (at the Bhandup factory and eventually at branches) anticipating demand and sending materials to the branches.

'Distinctive competence puts you so far ahead that the competition will find it difficult to catch up. We did that in dealer management [kitchen relationships], we did it in the supply chain, we did that in product innovation . . .' he told me. Acharya spent considerable time overseas (1985 to 2008) across China, Australia and other countries. In 2008, he returned to head the Asian PPG joint venture (discussed in the next section) before retiring in 2014. Acharya is currently the director and CEO at Paints and Coatings Skill Council.

Section 2: Foreign Collaborations

The 1980s were the first whiff of economic reforms before the big bang liberalization of 1991. The paints industry was getting ready for foreign tie-ups and expansions. While Asian Paints was number 1, its dominance was led by decorative, and the company did not have a large presence in industrial (which includes industries, auto, marine). The auto industry was set for a boom with Maruti Udyog being incorporated in 1981.

Expanding Presence in the Automobile Segment

As mentioned in the previous chapter, the passenger car industry had[6] only three players—Hindustan Motors, Premier Auto Industries and Standard Motor Products in Chennai. Two-wheelers were dominated by Bajaj Auto. After the original equipment manufacturer (OEM) business was the large after-market for repairs which was populated by small garages across India.

In 1978, Asian Paints launched Krilo, an acrylic automotive finish which was received well in the market. However the broader industrial segment of the paints industry was being served by companies like Goodlass Nerolac, British Paints and ICI, given their background with foreign partners.

With the opening up of the automobile sector, Japanese and Korean auto majors were set to enter India in a very big way from the 1980s right through to the 1990s. The first wave included Suzuki with Maruti, Honda with the Kinetic Group, and Daewoo with DCM. The second wave included Toyota with Kirloskar and Hyundai (100 per cent subsidiary) in the 1990s.

Japanese automakers at that time preferred Japanese paints suppliers, and two large Japanese paints majors entered India, tying up with the then top two paints players in India. In 1983, Kansai Paints entered into a technical collaboration

---

[6] R.C. Bhargava, *The Maruti Story*.

with Goodlass Nerolac (a precursor to them eventually buying a controlling stake from the Tatas in the 1990s), and in 1985 Asian Paints entered into a technical collaboration with Nippon Paints, Japan.

Berger Paints already benefited from being part of Hoechst AG, which had automobile paints technology. So, all three Indian paints majors would eventually become ready with paints for the automobile segment. A table listing the various collaborations that Asian Paints entered into with foreign players is given in Appendix 5.

Here is why these collaborations were important:

How Did Technical Collaborations Work in that Era?

The first task was finding the partner (usually a foreign company that owned a specific technology) and starting negotiations. Once the partner was found and terms agreed upon, an agreement for a specific period was signed which had to be renewed depending on the tenure (say after every three years or five years). After that, the Indian company (purchasing or licensing the technology) had to spend significant time and efforts to:

a) absorb and indigenize the foreign technology into their operations, which could require modifications to factories;
b) standardize products to comply with OEM/client standards and;
c) invest in hiring manpower to lead industrial/auto/marine divisions which requires a very different skill set than home decorative.

For example, the industrial division runs on contacts and relations with the OEMs in a very competitive market versus the home decorative segment where salesmen can directly approach dealers.

What Were the Areas of R&D with the Technical Collaboration?

a) Development of new products and processes through innovations in surface coating materials and intermediates;
b) Upgradation of existing products and technology with regards to quality and cost reduction of input materials;
c) Absorption and indigenization of imported technology;
d) Development of various industrial and high-performance parts to meet specific requirements of OEM customers, and
e) Development of tailor-made products for export markets.

What Were the Benefits?

Asian Paints invested around 1 per cent of turnover every year in R&D in the 1980s and 1990s. The main benefits (listed in Appendix 5) of this investment were in the form of new products and new clients that were developed by Asian Paints. Over and above this, there was improvement in processes and quality upgradations in existing products like Apcolite Royal, Apca automotive refinish paint, etc.

A Transformation in Thirty Years

Thus, Asian Paints embarked on an ambitious expansion spree in the 1980s, propelled by its #1 status, backed by the depth in managerial talent, and led by the second generation taking charge. In each decade, the company kept growing faster than the previous one, as seen in Table 10.2; the most significant jump, almost tenfold, was in the 1980s.

As seen in the table the sharp jump in equity capital in 1982 was because of the IPO, possibly the last significant event under the chairmanship of Champakbhai and before the transition to the second generation. We discuss both the IPO and the transition in the next section.

Table 10.2: Asian Paints Balance Sheet from 1962 to 1992

Rs in crores	1962	1972	1982	1992
Equity share capital	0.2	1.0	5.7	12.4
Reserves and surplus	0.2	0.9	8.5	88.7
Borrowings	0.4	1.5	5.3	80.5
Total	**0.8**	**3.4**	**19.5**	**181.6**
x (times)		4.2	5.7	9.3

(Source: Annual reports)

Section 3: Initial Public Offering (1982)

There was an IPO boom in the 1980s in India. In FY1981–82 alone, Rs 598 crore was raised[7] via shares and debentures (by non-government, public limited companies)—more than the Rs 548 crore raised cumulatively from 1977 to 1980. Prior to this, multinational companies like Ponds, Hindustan Lever, etc. offered[8] their shares at low prices to the public to dilute foreign holdings, as per FERA requirements discussed earlier in the book. In November 1977, RIL offered 28.2 lakh shares at par (Rs 10) to the public for the very first time. RIL's issue was oversubscribed[9] 7.19 times and is largely credited with creating the equity cult in India.

This was the era of the famous Controller of Capital Issues (CCI) when IPOs were notoriously underpriced (including for Asian Paints as we will see) to encourage and protect small investors but with the unintended consequences of creating price-rigging cartels of brokers in collusion with promoters.

[7] SEBI Handbook of Statistics (2004), Table 11, p. 17.

[8] ET Contributors, 'India's IPO Mart Has Changed; What Hasn't Is Investor Greed', *Economic Times*, 28 June 2017, https://economictimes.indiatimes.com/markets/stocks/news/indias-ipo-mart-has-changed-what-hasnt-is-investor-greed/articleshow/59350597.cms?from=mdr.

[9] Reliance 1977 annual report, p. 6.

The Sensex was constituted in 1986, with the base of 1979 as 100. The original thirty constituents of the Sensex are given in Appendix 1 and give an interesting insight into the largest industries and family-owned businesses in the 1980s—a topic we will visit later in the book. For the record, Asian Paints was included in the Nifty[10] in 2012 and Sensex[11] in 2015.

In 1982, Asian Paints received approvals from the CCI and launched its maiden IPO and the only time, so far, that the company has approached public markets for an equity issue. 'I recall doing many investor roadshows in that era along with Chari and Bipinbhai Jhaveri,' Atul Choksey told me. Roadshows are typically meetings between companies and investors organized by investment bankers for the issue. In that era, while there was[12] only one mutual fund, namely Unit Trust of India, there were other domestic institutional investors such as Life Insurance Corporation (LIC), etc.

Another feature of that era was that companies could advertise for the IPOs, and Asian Paints rightly capitalized on Gattu's popularity to highlight its blue-chip credentials. The print advertisements reveal a confident company inviting the public to take part in its success. Asian Paints was positioning itself on par with the multinationals (such as Sensex constituents, Nestle, Glaxo, Hindustan Lever and Philips) that were known for consistent dividends and bonus issues and whose IPOs were a bonanza for shareholders in the 1970s and the 1980s. For text and data from the ads, please refer to Appendix 4.

---

[10] 'Asian Paint, Bk of Baroda to Replace RCom, RPower in Nifty', Moneycontrol, 15 March 2012, https://www.moneycontrol.com/news/business/stocks/-1951119.html.

[11] 'Adani Ports, Asian Paints to Be Added in Sensex on Dec 21', Moneycontrol, 21 November 2015, https://www.moneycontrol.com/news/business/markets/adani-ports-asian-paints-to-be-addedsensexdec-21-1422699.html.

[12] 'Association of Mutual Funds in India', © Project 2016, https://www.amfiindia.com/investor-corner/knowledge-center/history-of-MF-india.html.

The ads reveal some interesting points. There were four hooks to tag lines which showed the compelling investment opportunity:

1) An existing blue-chip company ('Which paint company offers you a gilt-edged equity investment on a silver platter?')
2) The global reach ('Which paint company has put India on the world map?')
3) Consistent growth in profits ('When Asian Paints profits have gone up twenty-seven times in twenty years what's in it for you?')
4) A track record of paying dividends and issuing bonus shares ('How many paint companies have issued Rs 3.40 crore as a bonus on an original equity capital of Rs 10 lakh?')

A Large Base of Equity Shareholders

Just as Asian Paints created a large network of dealers in its early days, Champakbhai and the founders wanted to create a large network of shareholders as well. Champakbhai's belief in the family meant that employees and dealers would also be part of the issue. The government and stock exchanges laid down a minimum size of the IPOs to ensure the liquidity of stocks. Asian Paints went a step further and approached the Bombay Stock Exchange to increase the minimum offer size to 32.5 per cent of its post-equity base from 25 per cent as laid down by Rule 19(2)(b)[13] of the Securities Contracts (Regulation) Rules, 1957.

Thus, Asian Paints offered 16,85,185 shares priced at Rs 23, which consisted of a face value of Rs 10 per share and a share premium of Rs 13 per share. This included 84,259 shares (or 5 per cent of IPO size) reserved for employees and 33,704 shares (or 2 per cent) reserved for the business associates of

[13] 'Minimum Public Shareholding' https://www.taxmann.com/bookstore/bookshop/bookfiles/sample chapter23.pdf

the company. The remaining 15,67,222 shares were offered to the public.

The Asian Paints IPO was a large one, both in terms of percentage (32.5 per cent of post-IPO equity capital base) and in absolute terms (Rs 3.9 crore versus its 1981 balance sheet size of Rs 15 crore). To put things in perspective, RIL's offer size was Rs 2.8 crore in 1977. More importantly, RIL's offering was[14] an offer for sale (OFS) as part of stipulations with financial institutions who had lent it money versus Asian Paints which was a fresh issue of shares and expansion of capital base.

At the offer price of Rs 23, Asian Paints shares were valued at a ridiculous 4.5 times FY1981 earnings of Rs 5.07/share—that is how low the pricing was in the CCI era. DSP Financial Consultants ('DSP') were the lead managers for or of the Asian Paints IPO. DSP was led by Hemendra Kothari, one of India's most respected,[15] veteran investment bankers. The Asian Paints IPO, expectedly, got an overwhelming response, being oversubscribed ten times and the non-resident portion nearly twice. The allocation was made in October 1982 and shows how IPOs resembled lotteries, with your chances of getting an allotment increasing with the size of the application.

The luckiest of the lot was the minimum application of fifty shares, for such an investor had a two in nine chance (22 per cent) of getting an allotment but if successful, they would be allotted twenty-five of fifty shares (50 per cent) applied for. Assuming such an investor had the immense foresight and discipline to not sell her shares for the next forty-two years, her rewards would be colossal.

---

[14] Reliance Industries annual reports 1977 and 1978.

[15] 'Interview with Hemendra Kothari of DSP BlackRock', Moneylife News & Vie, https://www.moneylife.in/article/i-am-an-organisation-builder-and-i-want-to-bring-that-skill-to-my-philanthropy-hemendra-kothari/5006.html.

28 Per Cent CAGR over Forty-One Years

Rs 230 invested in Asian Paints IPO in 1982 is worth Rs 55.3 lakh today—an astounding 28 per cent CAGR over forty-one years (1982 to 2023). This is because a) the ten shares in 1982 have multiplied to 1843 shares today after bonuses and stock splits done by Asian Paints since listing, and b) I have assumed a share price of Rs 3000 which is the rounded-off average of the past year's trading prices. So, 1843 shares x Rs 3000/share = Rs 55.3 lakh.

And this excludes the dividends paid by Asian Paints during this period. Indeed, the cost of the investment would have been recovered by way of dividends in less than a decade, since between FY83 and FY90, Asian Paints' cumulative dividends amounted to Rs 27.36/share; on top of this, there were two bonus issues, 3:5 in 1987 (which means three new shares for five old shares) and 1:2 in 1987. There are indeed very few consistent wealth creators in the Indian stock market, and it pays to stay invested in them in the long term—a core philosophy of Saurabh Mukherjea's bestselling book, *The Unusual Billionaires*.

A Family Heirloom for Bharat Puri

Other than retail investors, there were many Asian Paints employees and dealers who were also lucky enough to be allotted shares back in 1982. Champakbhai Choksey was well known for telling everyone he met—including the neighbourhood grocer—to buy Asian Paints shares. Many of them did.

Some employees did too. I spoke to one such employee—Bharat Puri who had an interesting story to tell. 'My job during the IPO was to go and tell dealers what a [equity] share or was and how to apply. As a management trainee, I was eligible only for 100 shares, whereas employees got 200 shares. Now, 100 shares meant Rs 2300 and my salary was just Rs 1500. So, my dad and grandad wrote identical letters to me saying, "Nothing doing, here is a draft for Rs 1150 [from each of them], you will apply for these shares. There is no question of you not applying, these shares are for you." Can you imagine that? Both of them sent me Rs 2300 to invest. Its value today is more than Rs 5 crore,' he told me. When I asked if he had sold the shares, he replied, 'I will never sell them. It's a family heirloom.'

Section 4: Transition to the Next Generation

The IPO also marked the beginning of a transition—a transition that happened with an unwritten agreement and consensus of all four families, in peace and harmony. The succession plan would have likely been put in place and agreed upon in advance. The transition was also logical, given the increasing size and prominence of Asian Paints now that it was a listed company, as well as its reputation as a company where professional talent prospered.

In 1984, after leading the company from its inception, both Champakbhai and Suryakantbhai retired from active management, Champakbhai as chairman and managing director and Suryakantbhai as managing director. Champakbhai retained the title of chairman and was retained as an adviser. Meanwhile, Atul Choksey and Ashwin Choksi were both elevated to the position of managing director on 15 April 1984. To quote two paragraphs (page 4) from the 1983 annual report:

> Your Directors are of the opinion that the Company is at a crucial stage of its development when the experience, insight and long range perspective of Shri Choksey would be of particular value. Accordingly, they have decided to retain him as Advisor while continuing to function as the Chairman of the Board.
>
> Your Directors have further appointed Sarvashri Atul Champaklal Choksey and Ashwin Chimanlal Choksi as Managing Directors of the Company for a period of five years with effect from 15 April 1984. The Directors recommend these appointments for your approval.

The two paragraphs leave little doubt. While all four families had equal stakes in Asian Paints, the Chokseys were first among equals—a phrase I have heard repeated by many ex-employees I spoke with. When it came to leadership, Champakbhai was at the helm. He was the chairman of Asian Paints right till the day when he sold his stake in the company in 1997 and passed away. Atul Choksey, who joined Asian Paints in 1973 and entered the board in 1979, became managing director in 1984. Ashwin Choksi, who was senior to Atul both in age and in being the first member of the second generation to join Asian Paints (in 1965), was also managing director. Atul and Ashwin would remain managing directors till 1997 when the Choksey family split.

From many conversations that I have had with ex-employees, it was apparent that Atul Choksey was the face of Asian Paints, something that would be repeated in the press in 1997. Even before 1997, this was evident in something as mundane as his presence in the photographs (of various important events like receiving awards and signing agreements) that appended the annual reports in the 1990s to the all-important IPO in 1982 when Atul met investors.

Atul also followed in his father's footsteps when it came to the industry. He was president of the Indian Paints Association from 1987–89, president of the Bombay Chamber of Commerce & Industry (BCCI) and associated with the Associated Chamber of Commerce & Industry of India.

Asian Paints' rapid expansion, both in terms of manufacturing and—as we see in the next chapter—as a brand, happened with Atul and Ashwin as managing directors. It is important to emphasize the importance of Champakbhai and Atul Choksey now so that we can appreciate the events of the final chapter in this book.

Part 5

Leaving on a High

Chapter 11

Mastering the C in FMCG

'The greatest thing to be achieved in advertising,
in my opinion, is believability, and nothing is more
believable than the product itself.'

—Leo Burnett

Colours are emotions. Homes are dreams come true. Paints combine both and hence are among the most advertised brands today. How did Asian Paints become a brand that evoked emotions from consumers? More simply, how did Asian Paints become an iconic and much-loved consumer brand? The story is a mix of exceptional advertising and innovations. The earliest ads were in the 1950s but the brand powerhouse came much later, backed by research and some exceptional ad agencies. This chapter looks at the transition of Asian Paints from a seller of paints to dealers in the 1950s to the leading consumer brand that it is today.

The Early Days of Ads in India

It is a random coincidence that the first paints company (Shalimar Paints) and the first advertising agency (B. Dattaram

& Co.[1]) in India both started in 1902. Larger agencies like JWT entered in 1929. Pre-independence-era ads were made[2] for a British audience and featured brands like Horlicks, Lux, Lifebuoy, etc.

In the 1950s, foreign companies like Shalimar Paints, ICI, British Paints, etc. were brand leaders in India. Even in Western markets, paint brands like Dulux (ICI), Luxol (British Paints), Snowcem, Robbialac (Jenson & Nicholson), etc. were featured in ads and were well-known brands. Since television had yet to come to India, ads were mostly in print (newspapers, magazines, etc.), radio, outdoor hoardings and movies in cinemas. A 1951 print ad by Shalimar Paints[3] titled 'Women of Elegance' featured a graceful woman in an opulent home with the ad reading, 'Women of Elegance are well aware that Shalimar Paint products are the answer to their domestic decoration, interior and exterior [. . .] Be Bright and Say . . . Shalimar Paint.'

From Commodity to Brand through Ads

In her book, *Branded in History*, Ramya Ramamurthy links the post-Independence early boom in industry and construction in the 1950s to the logical rise of ads in cement and paints. On the importance of advertising in this sector, she quotes veteran adman Kiran Khalap of Chlorophyll.in as saying, 'Every company has to take this leap and not focus solely on the middlemen. Normally, cement, paint, plywood tiles—all of these require the middlemen, so these companies would put their focus and all their money on this.'

---

[1] CII Blog, https://www.ciiblog.in/from-commodities-to-brands-the-story-of-indian-advertising/

[2] Et Online, 'The Most Iconic Campaigns in Indian Advertising', *Economic Times*, https://economictimes.indiatimes.com/advertising-marketing/the-most-iconic-campaigns-in-indian-advertising/slideshow/10979340.cms.

[3] https://twitter.com/ShalimarPaints_/status/1253596974936449024?s=20

Taking the examples of famous ads by Videocon and Kitply, Khalap said, 'This goes to prove that when the commodity wants to become bigger, the brand has to market directly to the end consumer. Your product has to be in the mind and heart of the person who pays the money or else you won't have the brand imprint because the dealer is finally interested in margins.'

The Legend of Gattu

In the 1950s, Asian Paints ran two successful ad campaigns, the first was for Tractor, its washable distemper, with the ad line 'Don't lose your temper, use Tractor distemper!' The second—Gattu—was a blockbuster success. Legend has it that Champakbhai and the founders approached veteran cartoonist R.K. Laxman to come up with a mascot for Asian Paints in the 1950s. The mandate was simple: create a mascot that can take paints to the masses. Chain-smoking for inspiration, Laxman saw[4] the image of a boy with a paintbrush take shape through the cigarette smoke. The final image was of a mischievous-looking boy with scruffy hair standing next to a can of paint holding a paintbrush—a silent tribute to the humble painter who painted our homes.

But what to name the boy? Since the four partners could not come up with an idea, they held a contest for the public to name the mascot with a prize of Rs 500. 47,000 entries came in. On 30 December 1959, the company ran an ad with the mascot springing out like a jack-in-the-box, holding a placard with 'Gattu' written on it.

The copy read, 'The management of Asian Paints have pleasure in announcing that the name "GATTU" has been selected as the winner for the "GIVE ME A NAME" contest.

---

[4] *Economic Times*, 'The Story behind RK Laxman's "Gattu Ke Papa" and Asian Paints', Economic Times Blog, 2 February 2015, https://economictimes.indiatimes.com/blogs/et-commentary/the-story-behind-rk-laxmans-gattu-ke-papa-and-asian-paints/.

SHRI B.N. RELE, 17, 2nd Carpenter Street, Girgaum, Bombay 4 and **SHRI D. S. ARAS**, Block No. 1, Shri Siddha Sadan, 123A, Sion West, Bombay 22, who have both sent in the name **"GATTU"** equally share the prize of Rs 500/' (Author's note: bold, uppercase emphasis is as per the ad).

In early print ads, Gattu would be doing mischievous things such as sneaking[5] behind a man and painting his head, with the ad line 'any surface that needs painting needs Asian paints'.

Gattu was a hit. As Ramamurthy writes, 'This mascot was used in television ads well into the 1980s and it helped bring in the commodity-led business of painters into the homes of end users. [. . .] The Gattu experiment was vastly different from what rivals at that time were doing.' She quotes K.V. Sridhar of SapientNitro saying that Gattu took a drab, commodity-led business, limited to its core users—painters—and made it relevant to the larger audience of homeowners.

Gattu was everywhere—from print ads to Asian Paints' annual report going all the way to ads for the IPO. Ads in the 1960s featured Gattu in various situations, from mischievously painting a bald judge's head to solving a wazir's problem, where the copy was a poem titled 'Gattu and the Worried Wazir' that read as follows:

> 'I am sunk' the Wazir cried out in fright, 'The King comes visiting our town tonight.
>
> He wants the whole town painted in an hour. But if the paint won't dry, he'll feel so sour'
>
> Said the impish boy, 'Wazir, why despair? My Asian Paints your town will repair'
>
> The houses he painted in red and green. The paint was dry with a wondrous sheen.

[5] Disha Bijolia, 'How India's Largest Paint Company Was Born during the Quit India Movement', Homegrown, 2 February 2023, https://homegrown.co.in/homegrown-voices/how-indias-largest-paint-company-was-born-during-the-quit-india-movement.

> 'This town' said the King 'my capital shall be'. 'My paint' said Gattu 'works wonders all can see!'

Gattu was a big success in establishing Asian Paints' name in households. More importantly, by featuring a painter, Gattu appealed to the masses and helped Asian Paints entrench itself with its dealers, particularly those in smaller towns and cities. As Ramaswamy writes in *Marketing Management*,[6] 'Asian Paints and Gattu almost become synonymous. In rural markets of North India, buyers who wanted Asian Paints used to ask for the "*bachha chaap* paint [the kid's paint]"; they never mentioned Asian Paints. The identification with Gattu was so strong.'

Gattu was also displayed prominently on paint cans and helped Asian Paints in the economy segment which would later feature brands like Utsav. Mascots would go on to become famous and over time, Gattu joined the most famous advertising icons in India such as Air India's Maharaja, the Murphy radio child, the Amul girl, Onida devil, etc. The paints industry had no bigger mascot than Gattu.

Foreign Brands = Urban-Centric Advertising

While Gattu appealed to the masses, Asian Paints' competitors continued their focus on the urban, premium segment. One of the most successful outdoor campaigns in the late 1970s was Jenson & Nicholson with, 'Whenever you see colour, think of us'. I spoke to veteran adman, Ambi Parameswaran, an IIT–IIM alumnus, with whom I have the honour of hosting 'The Last Brand Standing' podcast, where we discuss famous battles between brands. The author of eleven books, Ambi has a storied career in marketing, sales and advertising where he led FCB-Ulka

[6] Exhibit 12.3, Marketing Management 6e, V.S. Ramaswamy, S. Namakumari (2018).

from 2003 to 2013. FCB-Ulka was behind[7] another memorable campaign, the Nerolac ad jingle, '*Jab ghar ki rounaq badhani ho, deewaron ko jab sajana ho, Nerolac* [When you want to do up your house, when you want to decorate your walls, Nerolac] . . .'

Recalling that era, Ambi told me,

> 'In those days [1960s, 1970s, etc.] Asian Paints was not seen as an image leader. It was seen as a tough competitor with economies of scale. Other companies would depend on Asian Paints for price increases. They would ask CHC for a price increase and CHC would decide the quantum of the increase. So, CHC squeezed the market. But it was not a marketing company. It was a cost-efficient leader who understood the market and dealers very well. It was rumoured that Asian Paints had schemes like a hidden rupee coin in a can of paint that only the painter would find, but the contractor or the homeowner would not. The Calcutta-based foreign companies were the brand leaders with the premium brand. Asian Paints had Apcolite but they had yet to establish themselves in the premium segment.'

A switch to consumer advertising from corporate advertising would help Asian Paints close that gap and television provided that opportunity.

The Consumer Boom of the 1980s

Television changed advertising forever. Black-and-white broadcasts and an early proliferation of television sets happened in large cities in India in the 1970s. But it was the 1980s when colour television (specifically, the Asian Games in 1982[8]) and the early

---

[7] Ambi Parameswaran, *Nawab, Nudes and Noodles* (2016).

[8] *India Today*, '1982-Colour Television Is Introduced: Out of the Dark Ages', 25 December 2009, https://www.indiatoday.in/magazine/cover-story/story/20091228-1982-colour-television-is-introduced-out-of-the-dark-ages-741614-2009-12-23.

set of economic reforms and liberalization ushered in the era of consumerism and the Great Indian Middle Class. The combination of colour TVs and Sunday morning state broadcasts of epic shows like Ramayana (1987–88) and Mahabharata (1988–90) would hold entire households in thrall, uniting them in one room in front of one screen.

Outside of the home, decades of poorly produced consumer goods, from fans to cars, came to an end. Economic reforms[9] ushered in joint ventures and easier import of equipment, and television advertising brought a new era of consumption to a country starved for quality and quantity. As Professor Roy writes, 'the Maruti car, Hero Honda motorcycle, Videocon television, washing machines, Pepsi Cola, HCL computers, and Reliance polyester fabric were the star products of the 1980s. These goods embodied not only foreign technology, [but] also a different marketing strategy from before, one that required reaching out to the consumer directly through advertisements rather than through distributors and wholesalers.' An entire generational change was happening in India, not just at Asian Paints. The bigger economic reforms of the 1990s would dramatically expand the choices of Indian consumers and set the foundations for the India we know today.

Cometh the Hour, Cometh the Man

Bharat Puri was instrumental in driving Asian Paints' marketing successes during the era of consumerism in post-liberalization India of the 1990s. Puri scored major victories for Asian Paints such as the launch of brands like Apex (the first smooth exterior emulsion which came with a five-year warranty) and Royale (Premium Emulsion). He was so successful that by 1997,[10] Asian Paints gained leadership of the premium segment when Royale displaced ICI's Dulux. Puri and his protégé, the late

---

[9] Professor Tirthankar Roy, *A Business History of India.*

[10] J. Ramachandran and Jalaj Garg, 'Asian Paints Limited: Painting History', (2018, IIM Bengaluru).

Chandramouli Venkatesan (who unfortunately passed away[11] at a young age in 2020) drove the transformation[12] of Asian Paints from just a plain interiors company to an interior and exterior company.

In my conversation with Puri, he often recalled with admiration the freedom (and hence responsibility) that he enjoyed as a young executive and then manager at Asian Paints. This invigorative work culture, which Puri also left behind at Asian Paints, was key to the two major wins that were close to Puri's heart and to Asian Paints' success—advertising and tinting machines.

1. Advertising

At Ogilvy and Mather (O&M), it was Piyush Pandey's brilliance that created some unforgettable ads for Asian Paints. Pandey was moved[13] from client servicing into creative as copy chief in the 1980s when the advent of television in India would make regional languages important in advertising. Puri and Pandey are arguably behind some of the most iconic ads at Asian Paints. Their partnership started with the Hindi translation of 'celebrate with Asian Paints', that Pandey translated as '*Har Khushi Main Rang Laye,*[14] *Asian Paints*'.

Asian Paints and O&M created some path-breaking ads that firmly entrenched the brand in the minds of consumers.

---

[11] BrandWagon Online, 'Pidilite CEO Chandramouli Venkatesan Passes Away', *Financial Express*, 7 October 2020, https://www.financialexpress.com/business/brandwagon-pidilite-ceo-chandramouli-venkatesan-passes-away-2099838/.

[12] 'Get Schooled by Bharat Puri and Chandramouli Venkatesan', www.youtube.com.

[13] Bhatt, Shephali, 'What Does O&M's Piyush Pandey Make of His Protégés' Flight Away from the Ad Agency?', *Economic Times*, 23 April 2014, https://economictimes.indiatimes.com/what-does-oms-piyush-pandey-make-of-his-protgs-flight-away-from-the-ad-agency/articleshow/34102693.cms?from=mdr.

[14] Meaning: bring colour to your happiness with Asian Paints.

The Pongal ad, made by Rajiv Menon with music by A.R. Rahman, was so successful that it was spun off in other languages. The Mera Wala Cream ad was based on the insight that shade cards by paint companies never had the exact shade of cream that consumers wanted. So, Asian Paints introduced the Apcolite emulsion shade card with 151 shades. The superhit ad for this shade card had the famous line '*mera wala* cream!' and was run across different settings like '*mera wala* blue', etc.

Vispy Doctor, the founder of Ormax Consultants, the consumer understanding agency hired by Asian Paints to explore the idea of increasing the number of shades on their shade card, told me, 'Asian Paints started thinking not in terms of chemicals or paints, but in terms of consumer—the "C" in FMCG. It's a very unique company.'

2. Tinting Machines—Asian Paints ColourWorld

A history of colour tinting machines (CTMs) is given in Appendix 1 on the paints industry. As marketing head, Puri launched CTMs under the brand ColourWorld for Asian Paints in 1997. The colourants were developed in-house, instead of the industry practice of using imported colourants—after all, Asian Paints had developed Majiktouch just twenty years ago. Puri went to the National Institute of Design (Ahmedabad), developed a full Indian shade card with 1000 shades, and worked with Corob (Italy) on the machines. Puri's team at Asian Paints worked with a design studio (Tesseract, Bengaluru) on a 'shop in shop' concept. The final product, which went on to be a hit, was rolled out as 'Asian Paints ColourWorld' and backed by a roadshow across the country.

An Environment of Freedom to Excel

Puri had all the freedom from the founding families to execute his plans. When I asked him about the Chokseys, he told me,

'I reported to Atul Choksey. He was the big picture person, very supportive and a natural entrepreneur. He could see the potential of what I was doing. I firmly believe that one of the reasons why, as such a young man, I got responsibility and moved up so fast was because he [Atul Choksey] could see what I was doing and gave me freedom.

'Here is one example: In those days, the rule used to be that if you made it in Asian Paints and you want[ed] to [move up to] be a general manager, you had to go and handle a factory. So, I was congratulated and told that I was being made head of the Ankleshwar factory. And I thanked them and declined the offer. They said I was making a move that would limit my career. I told them that I followed a simple philosophy—I must get out of bed and want to come running to the office. A factory did not excite me. I did not get my thrills from man-days per ton, manufacturing processes, etc.

'The seniors told me I was ruining my career. But Atulbhai told them, "Let it be, he knows what he is doing. Why are you guys insisting?" That's how I became the youngest head of sales and marketing. Can you imagine? At the age of thirty-four or thirty-five, I was head of marketing of the largest paints company in India!'

When I asked what that was like and how he ran a team of people much older than him without friction and with remarkable results, he said:

'If you asked me what my key strengths are, I would tell you two things. First, the ability to move consumers and second, the ability to get people to do things. Asian Paints was the foundation for me to develop these skills. And the freedom that I got came with responsibilities. For example, my team would work on our presentations through the night, so that they were perfect, and present the next day at sales conferences without having slept at all. That was the effort needed and we did it happily.'

Finally, we spoke about Champakbhai.

> 'In 1987, when I moved to the head office [Nirmal], Atul-bhai was in charge and Champakbhai had retired [from day-to-day activities] so I didn't interact much with him. But one day, he called me and asked, "Bharat, do you know anything about lasers?" Now Champakbhai isn't even an engineer, but I had to show that I knew something. I was an avid quizzer, so I told him, "Champakbhai, it means light amplification by stimulated emission of radiation." He said, "You know, I've been thinking, we take twelve to fourteen hours for paint batches in our mills, can we put a laser and get it done in one hour? Can you talk to Tirodkar at the factory about this?" I was amazed that there he was, always thinking about the company.'

He also told me about his conversation with Chari when Champakbhai passed away and the Choksey family sold its stake, 'So, I went to Mr Chari and asked him how I was to handle the ads during this change? Mr Chari was an upfront, outstanding gentleman. He said, "Bharat, we work for Asian Paints. We will do what is in the interest of Asian Paints." I told him I needed no further instructions.'

Puri left Asian Paints in 1998 to head sales and marketing at multinational confectionery giant Cadbury (later Mondelez).

Chapter 12

The Exit of the Chokseys

'The legacy of heroes is the memory of a great name and the inheritance of a great example.'
—Benjamin Disraeli

Asian Paints' achievements are staggering and defy convention. Why then did Champakbhai leave the organization after fifty-five years of playing a major role, in a company that he loved and helped build? The last chapter of this book tries to answer a question that only Champakbhai could have conclusively answered, a quarter of a century ago. Before you continue, I urge readers to read Appendix 7 on the family business construct in India, given that this chapter will deal with the split between the founding families in 1997.

Based on the interviews I've done with ex-employees, with industry experts and news reports of that era, I present two broad theories on the reasoning of the split. To this, I add a third point of view, that of Champakbhai's son and the last managing director from the Choksey family at Asian Paints, namely Atul Choksey. Atul spoke to me candidly and for the exclusive purposes of this book and I carry my interview in its entirety (edited for brevity and clarity).

I present all three perspectives as to why Champakbhai sold his stake in Asian Paints.

Theory 1: Fallout over Expansion, Funding and Diversification

The most popular theory around the split is a disagreement between the Chokseys and the remaining families regarding expansion of Asian Paints. Here are two accounts on the record, from a global perspective:

- Steven Irvine, Asia editor, *Euromoney*, wrote a detailed blow-by-blow account on the turn of events at Asian Paints in a 1 October 1997, article[1] titled, 'Hostile Buyers Beware'. In Irvine's version, the Chokseys fell out with the other families over a range of issues, including the issue of global depository receipts (GDR) to fund an aggressive expansion and allocation of board seats.
- Business journalist and author, Geoff Hiscock wrote a book in 2007 titled *India's Global Wealth Club* where he profiled Ashwin Choksi, then chairman of Asian Paints. In the profile, Hiscock wrote, 'Company co-founder Champaklal Choksey, who set up Asian Paints in a Mumbai garage with his three friends Chimanlal N. Choksi, Suryakant C. Dani and Arvind R. Vakil, began the sale process after falling out with the other families over a global rights issue in 1990 when he was chairman.'

Could disagreements over expansion really have been the reason behind the rift, as claimed above? One senior ex-employee I spoke to called it 'humbug', stating that there were 'no policy differences between the [four] families'. There were many employees who interacted with Champakbhai in those last few years and not one of those that I spoke to admitted

---

[1] Anonymous, 'Hostile Buyers Beware', Euromoney, 21 May 2016, https://www.euromoney.com/article/b1320dkshm7wtg/hostile-buyers- beware.

that they saw the split coming or that there were differences on the plans for expansion and their funding thereof.

We have spent the previous two chapters on Asian Paints' expansions and diversifications, which were comfortably financed by debt and internal accruals and in consensus with all the families. All of these even happened during the transition of first generation to the next with Atul Choksey and Ashwin Choksi becoming managing directors in 1984 and Champakbhai retaining the chairman's post. Many ex-employees credited Atul Choksey with leading these expansions and ventures and agreed that relations between the second generation were normal.

Was there an even more aggressive expansion plan to be funded by a GDR issue? I could not ascertain this for a fact from the employees I spoke to or from the media articles from that era. There were plans for a fifth plant in Maharashtra in FY1997 which were halted in FY1998 (after the Chokseys left) but surely that could not have been the single bone of contention?

The Diversification that Never Went Through

However, in the mid-1990s, there was a feeling (among employees) that the company was 'drifting' and was 'directionless', even if it was doing well financially. There were diversification plans, though, that never saw the light of day.

As per my conversations with ex-employees, there were plans at the top level for unrelated diversifications into products like steel, cement and ceramic tiles. Alarmed at these plans, a few senior employees rallied around Chari who said that CHC himself was not in favour (of the diversifications) but he (CHC) also knew that 'he was no longer in charge'. Finally, the idea of hiring a management consultant was floated, although Chari warned that CHC would not like the idea of an outsider critiquing the company.

Nevertheless, three management consultants were shortlisted to guide the company. All three were respected and reputed.

Two had worked with family businesses, like Asian Paints. The third was a leading multinational consultancy firm.

All three consultants held meetings with the promoters and senior managers and made initial pitches, wherein the multinational emerged as the most promising candidate. Their recommendation was against the diversification into unrelated areas which were under discussion. Their presentation was so compelling and exhaustive that the diversification plans 'were never heard of again', as one ex-employee put it.

Then came the final pitches by all three to Champakbhai, since as chairman, he had the final say. The first two consultants made no impact on CHC who thought the existing managers in the company would do a better job. The presentation by the partners of the multinational giant was kept for last.

After the partners presented, CHC thanked them and then asked them about another Indian client (an entrepreneur who had built a popular brand), whom the consultancy had recommended to sell his business to a large global competitor who was entering India. CHC asked the partners why they had recommended selling. The partners from the consultancy explained their rationale to CHC, that the Indian company would not be able to survive the incoming multinational's onslaught.

CHC made two observations: 'If you think the business was worth just X [the sale consideration recommended by the consultancy] then you don't know the value of that entrepreneur and his company, and my respect for you would be far higher if you had shown him how to beat the global giant in India, not how to sell out. Asian Paints is made differently. We have beaten every foreign company that was here. You should have told him how to beat the global giant. You're a reputed management consultancy. He didn't need you to tell him to sell out.'

That was the end of the meeting, and the multinational knew they had lost the account. While that management consultant was not hired, the plans for diversifying into unrelated items were also dropped.

So, how strong is the reasoning that differences like expansion (domestic, overseas, etc.) and funding for the expansion (GDRs, right issue, etc.) were the two reasons for the split? Probable and possible and left in the realm of speculation. We will never know for sure. But in the next section, we discuss the theory put forth by a few employees I spoke with.

Theory 2: Fallout over Transition

In 1997, Champakbhai was the last remaining founder of the first generation (Chimanbhai passed away in 1987 and Suryakantbhai in 1994), and it was obvious to many senior employees that a succession plan was needed. Given how friendly he was with the senior staff, they felt confident enough to approach him to have the 'difficult conversation' about who would lead the company after him. In these conversations, one thing was clear—Champakbhai had doubts about how the second generation would manage relationships between themselves, specifically the leadership (chairman, managing director, etc.).

One senior ex-employee floated the idea of an independent chairman who was reputed and respected such as eminent jurist, Nani Palkhivala whom Champakbhai knew and who had then visited him to present a book. Champakbhai was in favour of a committee of people and was reported to have said, 'When one man is not up to the task, we need to have a group of people to share the load.'

The culture at Asian Paints had also naturally evolved to being internally managed by professionals (led by Chari) with an external public face (then perceived as Atul Choksey). It was a well-oiled, well-run machine that consistently delivered and had hence moved beyond the contribution of one person or of four families.

This culture had evolved so well over the years that there was no doubt at all to the first or the second generation that the professional cadre would put Asian Paints above its founders. 'You did what is right for the company', was among the most frequently repeated lines I've heard in my conversations from employees who had spent thirty-plus years working at Asian Paints. Hence at that time, it was well accepted that Atul Choksey was the face of the company and that it was run by many professionals who were not related to the families of the founders.

Atul Choksey's Views

What was Atul Choksey's stand? I spoke to him at length, and he was willing to give his point of view on the split which happened twenty-six years ago. He told me,

> 'The decision did not happen overnight. My father believed that before the third generation entered the business, the families should be out [of active management]. He had seen other families go down the drain due to differences [within the family] and he had always taught us that the company was not our property. The house that we are living in might be our property. But the business belonged to all the shareholders. We could not treat it as an extension of our families, which many families were doing in those days.
>
> 'For two to three years, these discussions were going on [with the second generation of all four families] on what we should do. We cannot allow the third generation to come in and head this business. He [Champakbhai] thought we should professionalize the company. By then, Madhukar's touch was gone, but Chari was there, Abraham was there. So, he said we had to get good professionals and [if they stayed on with the company] we would promote them internally. After five to ten years, we could hand over the company to these professionals and make them responsible for performance. This was his rough idea. But the other families could not support this thinking.
>
> 'And he knew his sons would back him in this decision. He was very confident and assured with us [i.e., his sons Girish, Atul and Amit] since by then we had our specific businesses to run, namely, HMP, Choksey Chemicals and Apcotex.

> A road map to handing over the company also made sense at that time because by then Asian Paints had achieved a large degree of professionalism. There was a proper hierarchy and leadership and appropriate decisions were taken at the right time.
>
> 'We then decided that we would focus on our other businesses and not shoulder the responsibility [of seeing the company not perform]. That was how we decided to look out for buyers for our stake.'

Speaking about his father's unexpected death, Choksey added, 'The transaction took place on 31 July 1997. My father was so happy at finally letting go of this huge responsibility, of carrying this load on his shoulders that unfortunately, he passed away at our house in Pune. That was a historic day in more ways than one.'

My Takeaways from these Perspectives

Of the three perspectives presented above, I believe in the second theory, that the split happened over differences in who should lead Asian Paints. The popular first theory of disagreements on expansions and fundraising sounds plausible but improbable given that Asian Paints had a consistent track record of aggressive expansion and hiring top-notch talent—all four families had enough trust among them to back and believe in Atul Choksey and Ashwin Choksi's (both of whom were managing directors then) vision.

Funding for the expansion could have been a minor niggle but not a breaking point given Asian Paints' strong balance sheet and market leadership. Asian Paints had also become the institution that Champakbhai and his partners had envisioned. There was a large and robust management cadre that ran operations like a precision machine. This large bench of professional talent firmly believed in the vision of all four families, led by Champakbhai. As hindsight proves, they also believed in the leadership of the remaining three families, since there was no major exodus after the Chokseys' exit.

The bone of contention, thus, had to be who leads Asian Paints. It is possible that the expansion theory was a conduit to bring out differences between the family that had been festering for a while now that Champakbhai was the only remaining founder of the original four promoters.

A major decision like leaving your largest investment and your biggest success does not happen overnight, so it is reasonable to assume that—and as Atul Choksey alludes to above—the decision to exit was being thought over for a very long time. The other two alternatives—namely, the Chokseys buying the other families' stakes or vice versa—were probably impractical. Recall that a) each stake was then worth upwards of Rs 100 crore, a gigantic sum in that era, and b) for a business family to fund a large acquisition was an expensive proposition in terms of funding in an era where neither private equity nor venture capital existed in the bountiful way that it does today.

Champakbhai had seen enough family business splits and knew that the chances of a split happening in the next generation were very high. There were four families and the third generation would join in the next decade. Now in his eighties, Champakbhai knew how the story ends and it was not something he wished for a company that he gave his life to. He also knew that he could not acquire a majority stake in Asian Paints. Thus, an exit made sense.

Postscript: Asian Paints after the Chokseys

In the twenty-five years (FY1998 to FY2023) since the Chokseys left Asian Paints, its sales have grown thirty-seven times, profits sixty-one times, and market capitalization 237 times. One of the reasons that Asian Paints has prospered is that the remaining founding families have given full freedom to professionals to run the company—something that is rare among Indian families and hence to the credit to the promoter families of Asian Paints.

Chari had already been inducted on the board back in 1984 and stayed till he passed away in 2005. The role of managing director was ceded to a professional in 2009, just twelve years after Champakbhai passed away. Murty would be followed by K.B.S. Anand and then Amit Syngle. Their performance is evident in the numbers mentioned above. The strong leadership is backed by truly independent directors on the board with a depth of knowledge and experience. Indeed, the chairman of Asian Paints, Deepak Satwalekar, is not related to any family and has been on the board since 2000.

To cede control of a company that he lived his life for and to see it grow in the hands of professionals proves Champakbhai right in the most conclusive way. He envisioned this idea back in the 1950s when Asian Paints hired J.M. Nadkarni as chief chemist, followed by Madhukar and Chari, and then he took one of the largest bets on MBAs—something that India Inc. does routinely today—in the late 1960s, earlier than most Indian promoters.

This, therefore, is Champakbhai's most enduring legacy in India's corporate history. He has shown that promoters need to hire top-notch professionals, empower them and stay involved at the board level in capital allocation decisions. This legacy is what Champakbhai has left behind, making him a titan in Indian business.

Epilogue

'I had an intuition. I had a strong urge to visit my father, so strong that I was moved to tears,' Rita Parekh told me. And I know that she doesn't cry easily. After all, she's seen as the strongest among Champakbhai's four children. She went on, 'My husband couldn't join me, but I knew that I had to go immediately. I took a train and went alone to Pune and spent time with Papa, Mummy and Masi, who were there. I felt happy and returned in a couple of days although Papa told me to stay longer. I had to come back and look after the kids.'

On 31 July 1997, a few days after he spoke with his daughter and on the day that he sold his stake in Asian Paints, Champakbhai passed away. 'Even today, I feel that I should have stayed back,' she told me.

'We were at home that night and suddenly got a call from Mummy. He had passed away at the Pune bungalow. It was raining very heavily that night so she told us not to come to Pune, and she would come to Mumbai. We left home at night and met the ambulance [that was carrying his body] midway at the Ghats,' Amit Choksey said. Rita Parekh sat in the ambulance throughout the journey back home.

Parul Choksey, Atul's wife, told me, 'I was the last person to talk to him in the night at around 10.30 p.m. He asked me how I was and how Atul was doing [since Atul wasn't keeping too well that day]. I told him he was fine. He told me that now that the shares were sold, everything would be all right. He told me that after we came back, we would celebrate.'

Champakbhai had spoken to Parul earlier, telling her to be ready because things would change at home once they sold the shares. 'He wanted us to be prepared for the future. So, it was quite shocking when Mummy [Ashvinaben] called us at 11.30 p.m. to tell us that he had passed away.'

'He had called me earlier in the day on that Thursday to tell me that he'd sold his shares in Asian Paints. He sounded very excited and happy and told me to join him in Pune,' Sunita Choksey, Girish Choksey's wife told me. Sunita's son Ankur told me, 'I remember that Thursday. Dadaji called me from Pune and was very happy. He told me, "Ankur, now you have to get it done, you have to create the next Asian [Paints]."'

One of the last family events that Champakbhai attended was his grandson Prashant's (Ankur's younger brother) wedding in 1996. 'Papa was very sick at Prashant's marriage but he was ready on time. He was in a wheelchair but he still stayed right till the end of all functions at both [Ankur's and Prashant's] weddings,' Sunita Choksey (and mother of Ankur and Prashant) told me. 'He was very happy at Ankur and Prashant's weddings,' she added.

Champakbhai Choksey passed away on 31 July 1997, just a few weeks short of eighty-one years, and on the day he sold the Chokseys' stake in Asian Paints. His strongest beliefs were family and work. He believed that companies must outlast their founders and should support the people who work in and with the company, from employees to dealers. He had immense faith in honesty and hard work—the only two things he looked for in people. At the same time, he knew never to be dependent on people, which is why he wasn't affected much when people left, especially Nadkarni and Chari. Instead of becoming wary of professionals, he doubled down on them, often taking up managerial tasks on his own—as we saw in the internal emergency of 1975.

He was loved and respected among the employees and workers of Asian Paints. From encouraging a young Fausto

Cardoso to go to Guwahati to praising Bharat Puri in supporting a dealer during difficult times, there are many stories of Champakbhai standing like a rock behind good people. He helped create a culture that fostered merit and talent. He received support for this from the other families and together, the founders transitioned from a small paints company populated by friends, family and community to a massive, professionally run institution.

At the same time, he never lost touch with the workers and was (along with Chari) instrumental in resolving labour disputes at the Bhandup plant. This goes back to the time when workers at the Foras Road factory would frequently visit him at his home in Tardeo. Champakbhai was a people person and his ability to handle people of different temperaments was a key strength. His presence was formidable given his height, physical strength, as well as keenly sharp eyes. He was charming and—when required—offensive as well with a famously bad temper that, thankfully, mellowed with age.

While many founders and promoters pride themselves on their business skills, Champakbhai was keenly aware first of his lack of technical skills (to make high-quality paints that could compete with foreign companies) and then managerial skills to grow the company. These decisions—and support for them from the other families—were central to Asian Paints' success. He was an outgoing person who took easily to leadership, from the chairman of Asian Paints' to various industry bodies.

Although for a few years, Champakbhai had differences of opinion with his father, in his father's last years, he affectionately cared for him and looked after him with love and care. He even brought him to Mumbai from Surat, to take better care of him.

Champakbhai lived life to the fullest. He enjoyed the birthday parties thrown by his family, especially those at milestones such as seventy-five years of age. He was comfortable being the centre of attention within his family, and while he allowed his family to spend on his party, he would frown on excessively high expenditure at these events.

He wanted a good life for his children and himself but he also knew that excessive greed for wealth could destroy families—he had seen a few examples that left an impression on him. His children were given every necessity when they were young but they had to earn the luxuries on their own. While he was attached to and believed in family, he also believed in detachment, which is why all his children lived separately from him but within the same building. In all my visits to Geetanjali and meeting the family members, this sense of togetherness and family values was evident.

Champakbhai left an everlasting impact on the third generation of his family, especially Ankur and Prashant Choksey since both spent their early years when Champakbhai was alive. Ankur and Prashant Choksey's college education and early decisions in their career were influenced by their grandfather. He was also influential in their thinking and approach towards business and life. 'As a child, he was this giant of a man to me before I saw him [more emotionally] as a grandfather, as I grew up and he aged,' Prashant told me. Champakbhai was both indulgent and accommodating as well as strict and loving with his grandchildren.

A tradition that both grandsons recalled was mangoes in summer. Every Sunday, a carpet would be laid out and Ankur, and Prashant learnt how to eat the mangoes with both their bare hands.

> 'We enjoyed our aamras puri and earlier written bhajiya. He told us to put ghee and dried ginger to get a better taste. At the same time, he was very disciplined. Dinner was at 7.30 p.m. sharp and all the grandchildren had to be there. We had to eat with our hands, just like him and we couldn't complain that we didn't like a particular vegetable. We had to eat everything that was given to us. When the intercom came to Geetanjali and if we played with it, he'd tell us that the telecom was for adults only and children had to climb up and down the stairs if they wanted to speak to someone,' Prashant told me.

Both Ankur and Prashant graduated from colleges in the USA in the 1990s. Whenever they visited home during term break, Champakbhai would be keenly interested in what they were learning in their studies. Even though Ankur and Prashant weren't the first to study abroad (Atul Choksey had graduated in chemical engineering at Illinois Institute of Technology in the 1960s), Champakbhai was worried about how Prashant (the first grandchild) would manage all alone. 'The first time I saw emotion in Dadaji was when Mom told me that he cried when he read my first letter,' Prashant told me. Champakbhai never put any pressure on his grandkids on academics or careers. 'He told us not to be worried if we can't settle in the USA, we'd always be welcome back,' Prashant told me.

Champakbhai was a well-read person and this is possibly one of the reasons why he got along so well with Chari who was very knowledgeable in many subjects. Both also knew how to handle people well, with Chari having a degree in industrial management. This equation was critical to Asian Paints' early success when Madhukar left in 1971. Champakbhai's favourite books were *The Godfather* (Mario Puzo), and his favourite character was Fitzwilliam Darcy from Jane Austen's classic, *Pride and Prejudice*. He loved leadership and his favourite historical figure was Rana Pratap.

He was a religious person as well and read the Bhagavad Gita. *Autobiography of a Yogi* by Paramahansa Yogananda was another favourite. He firmly believed that everyone has a higher purpose in life that he or she must pursue. Prashant recalls his grandfather as being spiritual and taking inspiration from Swami Vivekananda.

> 'He told me that whenever I faced a problem, I should look within. Eventually, I will find the answer. He gave his own example, that whenever he faced a problem, he would go back to his learnings from Swami Vivekananda on concentration and focus. He would drop everything, at times even food, and with single-minded focus search for the answer, which he

> would eventually get. He'd keep repeating to me—no matter what your problem is, just use your powers of concentration and focus and you will find the solution; and to always remember that I am an entrepreneur and I have a mission in life,' Prashant told me.

But Champakbhai was also keenly aware of the cost of his disciplined, single-minded, all-consuming desire to build Asian Paints into a leader.

> 'He used to tell us to be balanced. Don't build something so big that you forget everything. He said he wished he had a hobby, that he could play badminton, or golf, or tennis or any sport. He didn't join any club and he didn't socialize much [beyond his family]. He told us not to be like him. He encouraged us to have friends and have a balanced life. He told us there's no need to build a giant that will kill your personal life. He had to do that but we don't need to,' Prashant told me.

Finally, some of his central principles in life were: a) there are no shortcuts or alternatives to success in business—there is only one way and that is hard work; b) solve each situation with practicality and common sense; c) develop courage for transformation with time and adapt to the changing landscape. He believed that adapting with time was as necessary for any person as it was for an institution or a business. Champakbhai always gave the example of a cockroach, pointing to its many years of survival by adjusting and adapting to the changing environment while other giant creatures have gone extinct.

Champakbhai's life work was Asian Paints and it is only poetic coincidence that he passed away on the day that he sold his stake. There will, obviously, be questions and crystal-ball gazing on how things would be if the Chokseys had stayed on. The wealth creation alone will make an overwhelming story. But that is in the empty realm of speculation and idle conversation.

What is real is Champakbhai's legacy and that will stand the test of time. Asian Paints expanded exponentially after he and his son left, which is testimony to the strength of the foundations that Champakbhai built with his life's work.

* * *

What happened after the split? In the Choksey family, Girish and his sons were already at the helm of Hindustan Mineral Products and Choksey Chemicals, while Amit was leading Mazda Colours. Atul took charge of Apcotex Industries full-time. He was joined by employees at Asian Paints who had worked in the Apcotex division such as Rengachari, S.K. Lahiri, B.V. Manjunath, and a few others. Rengachari became managing director (1997 to 2001), followed by S.K. Lahiri (2002 to 2010) and finally Atul's son, Abhiraj (2011 till date). Atul remains chairman.

Appendices

Appendix 1

The Paint Industry

Section 1: History of Paints

If homo sapiens walked the Earth 2,00,000 years ago, then paints originated more than 1,00,000 years ago[1] when cave artisans made ochre. The word 'paint' traces[2] back to the thirteenth century and has Anglo-French (paint, *peint*) and Latin (*pingere* or to tattoo, embroider, paint) roots. When applied to surfaces, paints provide two basic functions—colour (or decorative) and protection.

Paints are a huge industry on their own and associated products include building materials (like cement), speciality chemicals (like adhesives and sealants), and industrial coatings (like epoxy, etc.) as well as home solutions (like tiles, etc.). Thus, paint demand is a function of overall economic growth. For example, the more cars that are sold or homes made, the more paint will be required. Painting cycles (i.e., painting a home again) can be anywhere from five to six years or higher, depending on factors like location, culture, etc.

Paints are very old in application and were first made by artists and workers. The Renaissance, for example, in Italy in the fifteenth and sixteenth centuries saw masterpieces like the Mona

---

1 Wilford, John Noble, 'In African Cave, Signs of an Ancient Paint Factory', *New York Times*, 13 October 2011, https://www.nytimes.com/2011/10/14/science/14paint.html.

2 https://www.merriam-webster.com/dictionary/paint accessed on 6 January 2024.

Lisa being created in the early 1500s. Mechanization developed[3] alongside the Industrial Revolution (1760 to 1840), and by the mid to late 1800s, paint factories had begun springing up across the US. After that, grinding and mixing technology using machines evolved rapidly and paints were being used for everything from cars to television.

As academician, Theodore Zuk Penn writes in his 1966 thesis,[4]

> 'Shortly after the [industrial] Revolution the demand for paints began to grow. Not only were painting materials becoming cheaper and more available, but people realized that it was useful as a preservative. Before this, paint was usually viewed as a luxury item, and its practical value was not recognized. It became apparent in the late eighteenth century, however, that not only the wooden parts of buildings but also stone and brick lasted longer when they were protected from decay and weathering by a paint film. [. . .] American manufacture of painting materials on an industrial scale really began in the first quarter of the nineteenth century.'

Paint manufacture has evolved rapidly through the years. Lead, for example, once used for its benefits such as to accelerate drying and anti-corrosion, is now banned in paints given its harmful effects on humans.

Section 2: Largest Paint Companies in the World

The paint industry has some of the oldest companies in the world. Almost all the top ten players have a rich history dating back to the late nineteenth century. Some of AkzoNobel's

[3] 'History of Paint - American Coatings Association', American Coatings Association, 28 September 2022, https://www.paint.org/about/industry/history/

[4] Theodore Z. Penn, 'Decorative and Protective Finishes, 1750-1850: Materials, Process, and Craft,' *Bulletin - Association for Preservation Technology* 16, no. 1 (1 January 1984), https://doi.org/10.2307/1493913. Available at https://www.jstor.org/stable/1493913

businesses are more than 200[5] years old, even though the current corporate form took shape in 1994. The top ten paint companies in the world are featured in the table below, and although the data is based on 2021 sales, the top three are significantly ahead of the others.

Table A1: The top ten paint companies in the world as per Coatings World

#	Name	Formed in	Location	2021 sales (US$ b)
1	PPG Industries	1883	USA	16.8
2	Sherwin Williams	1866	USA	13.9
3	AkzoNobel	1994	Netherlands	10.0
4	Nippon	1881	Japan	6.8
5	RPM International	1947	USA	5.5
6	Axalta Coatings	2013	USA	4.4
7	Asian Paints	1942	India	3.7
8	BASF Coatings	1865	Germany	3.6
9	Masco Corp	1929	USA	3.2
10	Kansai Paint	1918	Japan	3.1

(Source: Coatings World, 8 January 2022[6])

Section 3: Paint Manufacture

Paints are mainly made with pigments, resins, solvents and additives. Pigments provide colour, resins bind the paint to the surface, and solvents thin the paint so it can be applied on a surface. Additives are also used to improve the paint quality on

[5] 'About Us, AkzoNobel,' https://www.akzonobel.com/en/about-us, accessed on 6 January 2024.

[6] https://www.coatingsworld.com/heaps/view/10269/1/ accessed 6 January 2024.

parameters such as drying time, UV-resistance, etc. Varnishes are also coatings that are used for protective purposes but are transparent and hence different in terms of utility from paints. Paints are usually sold in liquid forms (hence tins, cans, etc.) and applied by a brush, and there are also spray paints (in cans), and powder coatings (spray guns) as well as sophisticated paint application machines for industrial coatings.

Pigments are in solid form (usually powder) that provide colour, opacity and protection. Pigments are found in nature (indigo plants, iron oxide, etc.) and the paints industry uses organic pigments (carbon-based compounds like phthalocyanine) and inorganic pigments (made from minerals such as titanium dioxide). Resins provide the gloss, sheen, durability and adhesion that are critical to paints. Resins can be of many types such as acrylic, alkyd, polyurethane, vinyl, etc.

Pigments and resins are mixed together in solvents such as water or oil to form the final product, i.e., water-based, oil-based, etc. When paint is applied on a surface, the water or oil dries out, leaving behind the colour. Additives are added for specific properties.

Paint manufacturing is a raw-material-intensive technical process that involves a high degree of precision; this is why paint factories have laboratories and chemical engineers. The main raw materials are pigment (titanium dioxide, zinc oxide, etc.), resins (alkyd, acrylic and epoxy, etc.) and solvents (turpentine, naphtha, etc.). The broad steps are as follows but will depend on the type of paint being produced.

- Raw materials are first weighed and then mixed using dispersers and mixers in precise proportions to form a pre-mix.
- The pre-mix is then milled down (ball mills, bead mills, roller mills, etc.) to reduce the size and mix easily with

the binder. The mixture is further mixed with binders, solvents and additives in a process called 'let-down'.

- The final product is subject to quality control checks, packaged into containers and sent off for distribution.

Section 4: Categories of Paint

Paints can be classified in many ways but the most common and easy-to-understand categories are decorative and industrial.

A. Decorative/Architectural Segment

The decorative or architectural category consists of paints used in homes, buildings, offices, etc. These are the various types of segments within the decorative business of Asian Paints as described in its 2023 annual report: interior wall finishes, exterior wall finishes, waterproofing, wood finishes, enamels, adhesives, tools and undercoats. The decorative business (including home decor) segment accounted for 88.2 per cent of Asian Paints' revenues in FY2023.

Varnishes, usually included with paints, are clear coatings usually made for wood surfaces. The distribution structure of the decorative segment (explained in Chapter 3) consists of a large network of dealers, distributors, retailers, etc. which buys from larger wholesalers and even directly from the company (via depots, stock points and even factories). In FY2023, Asian Paints had more than 1.5 lakh retail touchpoints in India in its decorative business segment.

Interior paints range from distemper at the lower end to emulsions at the higher end—both in terms of price points and durability. Asian Paints' range of interior paints are under the Royale, Apcolite and Tractor brands. Exterior paints need to be more durable and withstand the vagaries of weather and hence usually come with guarantees from the manufacturer. Asian Paints exterior paints are under the brands Ultima, Apex and Ace.

B. Industrial Segment

The industrial segment consists of paints used for protection of surfaces against corrosion, weather, rust, etc. Buyers can be original equipment manufacturers (OEMs) and large industries include automobiles (cars, trucks, two-wheelers, etc.), consumer durables such as refrigerators, washing machines, etc., all the way to governments (for public utilities like bridges). Paints and coatings in the industrial segment are, hence, specific to their industry. The paint used on cars cannot be the same as the paint used on a television.

Given their nature, the industrial segment runs directly between the paint manufacturer and industrial customer and, at times, staff from the paint companies are deployed at the customer's factory. There are strict quality norms that the paints company has to comply with which usually requires investment in constant technology upgradation. Kansai Nerolac is India's largest player in the industrial segment.

Section 5: History of India's Paint Industry

Paints were imported into India during the British Raj and sold by local traders, merchants, etc. For example, the earliest member of the Dhingra family (of Berger Paints), Bhai Uttam Singh Kesar Singh[7] began distributing paints in the late 1800s. In 1902, two Britishers, A.N. Turner and A.C. Wright, established Shalimar Paints, India's first paints factory in Howrah, Calcutta and the first such plant in Southeast Asia.[8]

---

7 Sonu Bhasin, *Unstoppable: Kuldip Dhingra and the Rise of Berger Paints.*

8 'About Us', https://www.shalimarpaints.com/about-us, accessed on 6 January 2024.

However, this lone factory could not do much in the early 1900s, in the absence of both raw materials and suppliers and distributors.[9] Thus, almost all of India's paints requirements were met by imports with no domestic manufacturing facilities. World War I gave a real boost to India's paints industry. The rise of the multinational group of industrialists was responsible for the paints industry's early origins in India, as we see in the next section.

As imports halted, the paint literally dried up. Marketing agents that imported paints from abroad looked to set up factories in India. Europeans (who had already established paints factories in Europe) rushed in to meet the demand from within India as well as for the British armed forces. Thus, the period between the end of World War I and the beginning of World War II saw the greatest-ever influx of foreign paint companies into India (Table A2).

As per the Indian Paints Association, by 1938, the annual production of all the paint companies put together is estimated to have been around 24,700 tonnes, reportedly 60 per cent of India's requirements at that point in time. However, the British dominated the paints industry and if there was a battle between India and Britain for independence, then even in the paints industry, Indian companies had to battle British companies for technology, raw materials, capital and distribution. It was thus a highly competitive and open market dominated by the British and Europeans who had deep pockets as well as a political system to back them.

As can be seen in the brief history column, all paints companies in India have seen significant ownership changes, except Asian Paints (barring the Chokseys' exit in 1997). A closer look at this relevant issue and how it played out in the case of Shalimar Paints and Berger Paints is discussed in Chapter 2.

[9] Anand Adhikari, 'Shalimar Paints Has Seen Three Ownership Changes', *Business Today*, 7 July 2011, https://www.businesstoday.in/magazine/cover-story/story/history-of-shalimar-paints-22808-2011-06-23

Table A2: The first paint operations in India (indicative list, not exhaustive) set up by foreigners

Company	Location	Year	Brief history
Imperial Chemicals Industries (ICI)	Calcutta	1911	- Brunner Mond opened trading office in 1911 - Name changed to ICI in 1929 - JV with Govt (Indian Explosives) in 1954 - AkzoNobel buys ICI in 2007 - Currently listed as AkzoNobel India
Goodlass Wall	Bombay	1920	- Acquired Gahagan Paints, Bombay - Changed name to Goodlass Nerolac (1957) - Became part of Tata Group (1976) - Currently listed as Kansai Nerolac
Jenson & Nicholson	Calcutta	1922	- Originally dates back to 1821, UK - Insolvency proceedings[10] in 2017 - Brand currently with Sheenlac Group (Chennai)

[10] Staff Reporter, 'Colour Drains Out of Jenson', *Telegraph India*, 4 August 2018, https://www.telegraphindia.com/business/colour-drains-out-of-jenson/cid/1478490.

Hadfields	Calcutta	1923	- Acquired by British Paints (1947) - Eventually became part of Berger Paints
Hoyle, Robson, Barnett & Co.	Calcutta	1923	Eventually acquired by J.K. Group
Elephant Oil Mills	Bombay	1937	- Started originally in oilseed crushing - Acquired and renamed as Garware Paints (1978)

(Source: The Indian Paints Association, company websites)

Section 6: India's Paints Industry in the 1950s

What was the paints industry like when Asian Paints was in its early days? The industry was split into extremes—at the lower end was the unorganized sector that then operated outside of the ambit of indirect taxes (like excise, sales tax, etc.). These small mills ran on basic technology and hence sold basic quality products. Since they did not come under the indirect tax ambit, their products were cheaper than branded products.

At the other extreme was the organized sector consisting of large companies, both foreign (Goodlass Nerolac, Jenson & Nicholson, ICI, British Paints, etc.) and Indian companies like Asian Paints. Over time, as indirect taxes were reduced, the price advantage for these companies was eroded and the organized sector became larger.

Demand for paints was usually led by government and industry, as the household demand was split across low-end chuna and high-end emulsion. In terms of value, the industrial segment was larger in the post-Independence era. Raw material supply, which was a major issue pre-Independence, had eased thanks to the efforts of industry bodies like IPMA.

The first Five-Year Plan from the Planning Commission dedicated four pages for the paints and varnishes industry. An extract from this section shows the state of the industry in 1951.

The plan also noted that the railways and engineering industries, including shipbuilding, were the most important consumers of paints. This implied that the wall-painting segment did not exist or was negligible.

Table A3: Overview of the paints industry in India in 1951

Total number of factories engaged in production of paints, varnishes and enamels	**150**
Of the above:	
- Very small in size	100
- Major in size	50
Of the above:	
- Units with capacity in Calcutta	18 units with 36,360 tonnes
- Units with capacity in Bombay	17 units with 19,860 tonnes
- All other major units across India	15 units with 8580 tonnes
- Total units with capacity	50 units with 65,000 tonnes

(Source: Indian Paint Association from the first Five Year Plan)

Section 7: Tinting Machines

Colour matching has a rich history going back to Pantone colours in the 1960s, and most of the technology has evolved only in the last fifty years. Colour television came into India only in the 1980s and newspapers went colour even later. In the world of painting, the task of finding the right colour for your home has always been a tough and very personal task.

Tints are colours mixed with white, shades are colours mixed with black, and tinting and shading gives tones. Anyone who has painted their home would have seen that a painter starts on a wall (usually a white wall) and makes tints and shades with combinations of pigments mixed in a base paint. These tints and shades are developed from colours called universal stainers which are concentrated pigments formulated to be compatible with various paints such as water-based, solvent-based, etc.

Asian Paints was ahead of the curve in colour matching. In 1979, a new computer-aided colour control system was installed to further product development and optimize usage of pigments which, as per Saurabh Mukherjea in *The Unusual Billionaires*, helped reduce tinting time from five or six days to four hours.

Also, in the 1970s as mentioned in Chapter 4, Pramesh Khanna developed the 'Asian Paints Majiktouch' concept in Asian Paints R&D lab at the Bhandup factory. This product was ahead of its time and would turn out to be the precursor to the tinting machines. Sold in the form of tubes, Majiktouch was an upgrade on the universal stainers. Majiktouch tubes were pre-mixed (in the right formulation) and sold as per the tint or shade they produced.

All the painter needed to do was squeeze the tube, mix it with a base paint, and get the tint or shade desired. Majiktouch tubes came with specific shades, thereby reducing the need for painters to experiment with universal stainers and yet go beyond the ordinary shade cards. Asian Paints was the first paints company with the Majiktouch concept which was probably ahead of its time.

Fast forward to colour tinting machines (CTM, also known as computerized colour dispensers or CCDs). As mentioned in the earlier chapter, CTMs were already being used in the Fiji Islands by paints dealers in the 1970s. What was a CTM and what problem did it solve? CTMs[11] tint multiple neutral bases, each designed to cover a range of colours, i.e., dark, medium or

[11] Saurabh Mukherjea, *The Unusual Billionaires* (2016).

pastel. This machine automatically tints the shade desired by the customer once the shade's code is punched in. As a result, the number of colour shades offered by the dealer at his shop increased dramatically from 125 colours to more than 5000.

CTMs were obviously a hard sell in India given the high installation cost[12] which the dealers were reluctant to incur. But the industry persevered and over time, CTMs became commonplace. In India, Jenson & Nicholson[13] in collaboration with Tikkurila OY (Finland) launched the Instacolour concept—a first in the paints industry—in 1995. The product received a very good response as the 1997 annual report states, 'Instacolour was introduced in two products and 626 shades. In a period of one year, we have been able to expand the product range to six and today the shades are over 2500.' Berger Paints followed suit with the launch of Colorbank in 1996 and made good progress. By 1999, Berger[14] had installed 400 tinting machines, out of 1200 tinting machines in the industry.

Section 8: What Lies Ahead

Since 2019, five companies have announced forays into paints, namely JSW Group, Astral Poly, JK Cement, Pidilite and Grasim. Of these, when the Aditya Birla Group's Grasim announced that it was doubling the capex for its paints foray, Asian Paints' and Berger Paints' stock price tanked.[15]

And Grasim is already testing out a brand of paint, Sparkle, among a closed set of users. In early 2023 at Davos, Kumar

[12] As high as Rs 8,31,000 as per Saurabh Mukherjea in *The Unusual Billionaires*.

[13] https://jnpl.in/history.html, accessed on 8 January 2024.

[14] Saurabh Mukherjea, *The Unusual Billionaires*.

[15] Livemint, 'Asian Paints, Berger Paints Share Prices Tumble as Grasim Doubles Capex Plan', *Mint*, 25 May 2022, https://www.livemint.com/market/stock-market-news/asian-paints-berger-paints-share-prices-tumble-as-grasim-doubles-capex-plan-11653473224113.html.

Mangalam Birla was quoted[16] as saying, 'When we announced our foray into paints, we said that we have a natural right to win—when I say "win", I don't mean against Asian Paints.'

Asian Paints has spent decades building up its competitive advantages and creating impressive moats against competitors. Just putting up capacity, therefore, will not be enough for any new player entering the industry, irrespective of how deep their pockets are, and pockets will matter. Asian Paints is significantly larger than the #2 player, Berger Paints, who also has formidable ownership in the form of the Dhingras.

Only time will tell how this battle plays out and the battle in paints is indeed happening after a long time. It took twenty-five years for Asian Paints to dethrone its competitor and become #1. It never rested on its laurels. Champakbhai and the founders kept placing block after block in front of their competition and stayed ahead consistently. Their values have endured even after Champakbhai left, and the company that stands today is ready for any battle that the future might bring to its doorstep.

[16] Sumant Banerji, 'Wet Paint Alert: Can Grasim Industries Surprise Berger Paints?', *Mint*, 13 June 2023, https://www.livemint.com/companies/news/can-grasim-industries-surprise-berger-paints-11686681332171.html.

Appendix 2

A Brief History of Management in India

Early Roots in the Managing Agency

The managing agency era in India (roughly 1834 to 1956, when the Companies Act was introduced) guided India's entry into modern industry, trade and commercial agriculture. By World War I, managing agencies controlled 75 per cent of the industrial capital of India and accounted for half the industrial employment. Here is how it worked: an entrepreneur started a managing agency after raising funds from friends, family, banks, etc. The agency would start a company and once it tasted success, the agency would sell most of its stake in the company to the public and move on to another business and follow the same model.

In each business, the agency would sign a long-term management contract with the company whereby it controlled management with only a small financial stake. Successful managing agencies—and the families that controlled them—thus had access to the resources of large companies and could attract the best (from a very limited pool) talent to run the companies. The companies, in turn, had the low costs of a lean, common management (across businesses), economies of scale, and access to common marketing networks.

In his book *Goras and Desis* Omkar Goswami writes,[1] 'With all these advantages, managing agencies were quickly successful, and the innovative structure became popular both with British *gora* and Indian *desi* business communities.' The idea was so successful that by the early 1930s, large managing agents controlled several widely held, listed companies in capital-intensive industries like jute and cotton mills.

However, as India achieved independence, the managing agency system—which now appeared like a relic of the colonial era—began its decline. More formal sources of finance (government-sponsored financial institutions like IDBI, ICICI and IFCI) widened access to capital. Managing agencies were formally terminated under the Companies Act, 1956. Managing agencies thus introduced the concept of separation of ownership and management in corporate India.

The Role of TAS in Training Great Professionals

In 1945, Jehangir Ratanji Dadabhoy 'JRD' Tata, the iconic chairman of the Tata Group, set up Tata Industries as the managing agency for Tata Sons. By this time, the Tata Group had expanded across industries from steel (Tata Steel–1908), to hotels (Taj Hotel–1903), to electricity (Tata Hydro Power–1910), to soaps (Tata Oil Mills–1917) and much more. To run all these companies and expand even further, it was evident that the Tata Group needed talent. In 1956, JRD set[2] up Tata Administrative System (TAS), the flagship leadership development programme of the Tata Group.

In a wonderfully detailed book, *Tata Leadership Experiment*, ex-TAS officers Bharat Wakhlu, Mukund Ranjan and Sonu Bhasin wrote about the origin and impact of TAS. TAS was

[1] Omkar Goswami, *Goras and Desis: Managing Agencies and the Making of Corporate India* (2016).

[2] Bharat Wakhlu, Mukund Rajan and Sonu Bhasin, *Tata Leadership Experiment* (2022).

designed to be like the Indian Administrative Services (IAS), an elite cadre of highly trained professionals working in unison for a common cause. JRD's vision was that the cadre would be the adhesive binding the diverse businesses of the Tata Group. TAS members would move across companies to work with senior leaders and make a wholesome impact. While multinationals had formal training and induction programmes, TAS was the first such rigorous internal management development programme by a large Indian group.

Outside of academics, companies were doing their own internal management training programmes. Besides TAS, the other significant effort in management development and research was Dr Vikram Sarabhai's Ahmedabad Textile Industry's Research Association (ATIRA), founded in 1947. Both JRD and Sarabhai were significantly ahead of their time.

The managing agency model and TAS are among the most significant early efforts of developing formal training in management in India. While the idea of a company is centuries old, the idea of an MBA is comparatively new. Commerce degrees were common in Indian universities, but these were hardly adequate for management. Till the 1950s, businesses in India were run[3] either by owners (and their families) or foreign-trained managers who ran the managing agencies mentioned above.

This is important to consider in the timeline of Asian Paints because in the 1950s and 1960s, Asian Paints was successful in recruiting chemists from UDCT and the contribution of people like Madhukar and Chari was having a visible impact. The birth of the IIMs at this time is the next milestone to consider. And there is a link between the Tatas discussed above and the birth of the IIMs as we see next.

[3] Bhavesh Patel, 'Management before the IIMs @ Archives', n.d., https://archives.iima.ac.in/firstdecade/Management-before-the-IIMs.html, accessed on 6 January 2024.

History of the MBA Degree in India

India's oldest management school is Xavier Labour Relation Institute (XLRI, now known as Xavier School of Management or XSM) which was set up[4] by the Society of Jesus in Jamshedpur with help from TISCO in 1949. XLRI started with management-centric courses for trade unions before launching a two-year, full-time programme in industrial welfare (later rechristened as Human Resource Management).

In 1948–50, Jehangir Ghandy, director at Tata Sons, chaired the Industrial Administration Business and Management (IABM) Committee set up by the Council for Technical Education. The recommendations of the committee included the creation of a board of management studies to facilitate university-level tie-ups, a national institute of management to oversee management education and an Administrative Staff College on the lines of Staff College in Henley (UK).

As an offshoot, the All-India Institute of Social Welfare and Business Management (now known as IISWBM) was set up in 1953. Several university departments also began to offer management programmes. Delhi University's Faculty of Management Studies (FMS) was set up[5] in 1954, and a three-year, part-time, postgraduate diploma course for working executives was launched in 1955.

A Brief History of the IIMs

Just as the rise of the paints industry spawned collectives like IPMA and Paints Federation, the rise of management education spawned management associations. The All-India Management Association (AIMA) was formed in

[4] 'XLRI–One of the Best Management Schools in India', n.d., https://xlri.ac.in/about/heritage.php, accessed on 6 January 2024.

[5] 'History', Faculty of Management Studies, n.d., http://www.fms.edu/?q=node/10, accessed on 6 January 2024.

1957 and its president, Charat Ram, approached Douglas Ensminger, a representative of the Ford Foundation in India, for assistance. Paul Hoffman, the first president of the Ford Foundation, had met Jawaharlal Nehru many times in 1951. Following his efforts, the Ford Foundation opened an office in Delhi with Ensminger as the foundation's representative in India. Ensminger[6] was a strong proponent of autonomous management institutes training fresh graduates outside of the traditional university system.

His interests aligned with the central government which began to appreciate the need for management education during the second Five-Year Plan which envisaged heavy industries in the public sector. After many consultations between the Ford Foundation and the Indian government, the idea of an autonomous management institute was approved.

Dr Vikram Sarabhai lobbied hard and won support for one institute to be relocated to Ahmedabad (from its originally intended location of Mumbai) and Humayun Kabir (of the Ministry of Scientific Research and Cultural Affairs) and his close friend, chief minister of West Bengal, B.C. Roy championed the cause of another institute to be located in Calcutta. The central government promised initial financial support while the respective state governments were to provide land. This is how the IIMs were born.

In 1961, two IIMs were set up, IIM Ahmedabad (IIMA) in collaboration with Harvard Business School and IIM Calcutta (IIMC) in collaboration with Alfred P. Sloan School of Management (MIT). Both IIMs started executive development programmes and flagship two-year programmes in business administration in 1964. Asian Paints visited the IIMA campus for the very first time in 1968.

---

[6] Bhavesh Patel, 'Dr. Douglas Ensminger and the Ford Foundation @ Archives', https://archives.iima.ac.in/firstdecade/Dr-Douglas-Ensminger-and-the-Ford-Foundation.html, accessed on 6 January 2024.

Appendix 3

A Brief History of Computers in India

Computers in India have a fascinating history, much of which has been recorded extensively in a project called Itihaasa.com (Sanskrit for history) which chronicles the history of computers and the Indian Information Technology (IT) sector. Founded by N. Dayasindhu and Krishnan Narayanan, the website is a treasure trove of resources on the history of India's IT sector. The founders, along with Infosys veteran, K. Gopalakrishnan have also written a wonderful book, *Against All Odds: The IT Story of India* on this topic which chronicles India's success in IT, ITES and related fields.

The Indian Statistical Institute (ISI) in Kolkata, led by P.C. Mahalanobis, and the Tata Institute of Fundamental Research led by Dr Homi Bhabha were among the first to use computers in India. These were either imported into India (HEC-2M for Rs 2 lakh from the British Tabulating Machine Company at ISI in 1955) or indigenously developed (TIFRAC at TIFR in 1962).

By the 1960s, the Indian market was large enough to attract international companies to assemble (not import, since that was prohibitively expensive and impractical) computers and sell them. There were two companies selling computers in India—the International Business Machines Corporation (IBM) whose most popular model (even called the Ford Model-T of computers) was the 1401 and International Computers Limited (ICL) with the 1901A. IBM was far ahead of ICL.

Computers at IITs

Here is how computers were adopted at India's premier colleges of engineering. IIT Kanpur was spearheading the effort in computer education with the first M.Tech programme starting in 1965, soon after an IBM 1620 was carted (literally in a bullock cart) into the campus in 1963. The IBM 1620 was followed by a mainframe, the IBM7044. By 1968, IIT Kanpur had two batch-processing second-generation computers—an IBM7044/1401 and an IBM 1620. The IBM 1620 was used to teach programming and the IBM7044/1401 was used by faculty and research students.

West of Kanpur, IIT Bombay was founded in 1961 with help from Russia, which also resulted in the first computer, installed in 1967, being a Minsk. I spoke with K.B.S. Anand, batch of 1977 at IIT Bombay, on using the Minsk and he told me, 'I spent days and nights at the computer centre doing my thesis. It was a slow computer and we had to learn a different language, ACE, for the computer. It wasn't very user-friendly.' In the book, *Against All Odds*, Nandan Nilekani, batch of 1978, IIT Bombay, described Minsk as 'a Russian machine EC1030 which was essentially like an IBM 360'.

Incidentally, the first computer[1] at IIMA was a novel Hewlett-Packard (HP) time-sharing computer system in 1970 which came as one of the last grants to IIMA from the Ford Foundation. The IIMA computer team was led by Prof. J.G. Krishnayya who had recruited a young Narayana Murthy (one of the founders of Infosys) from IIT Kanpur as a systems analyst. Veeraraghavan was in the batch of 1969 at IIMA, and while he narrowly missed out on using the HP machine, he had learnt programming languages while at IIMA. 'We had limited exposure to computers and learnt the basics, including languages like FORTRAN and how applications work,' he told me.

[1] Bhavesh Patel, 'Dr. Douglas Ensminger and the Ford Foundation @ Archives', n.d., https://archives.iima.ac.in/firstdecade/Dr-Douglas-Ensminger-and-the-Ford-Foundation.html, accessed on 6 January 2024.

Computers at India Inc.

Here is how computer adoption shaped out at Indian companies. In 1961,[2] IBM installed the 1401 computer at Esso in Mumbai, the first instance of a multinational selling computers in India, as stated in *Against All Odds*. Biji Kurien, who had worked at Esso, told me, 'The computer occupied the whole floor at the office in Nariman Point. Some of us were there for training but we had no access to the computer room. You could stand near the elevator and hear the whirring sound of the computer working with all the punch cards.'

But the first bunch of people open to the idea of computerization were, strangely enough, jute mill owners. IBM sold the jute mill owners a payroll processing service and the mill owners who could not afford the 1401, leased computer time from IBM to process their payroll. Once IBM entrenched itself as a payroll service provider, it branched off into inventory control and financial accounting services as well. Thus, by the 1960s, both computer hardware and applications were known to Indian companies, even though not many could afford them.

The Tatas were ahead. In the 1960s, the first Indian corporate computer services group was in Mumbai—the Tata Computer Center in 1967, which would eventually be hived off as Tata Consultancy Services (TCS). S. Ramadorai who retired as CEO and MD of TCS in 2009, after serving the company for thirty-nine years, wrote *The TCS Story . . . And Beyond* in 2013 where he states, 'By 1968, TCS had two IBM 1401s on lease and one ICL 1903 which was purchased. All these were housed on the eighth floor of Nirmal Building and nicknamed Able-Baker-Charlie.' It is indeed a quirk of fate that TCS (eighth floor) and Asian Paints (fifth floor) were neighbours at Nirmal Building, Nariman Point.

[2] Kris Gopalakrishnan, N. Dayasindhu, Krishnan Narayanan, in their book *Against All Odds: The IT Story of India* (2022).

Appendix 4

The Original Constituents of the S&P BSE Sensex as on 2 January 1986

Name of Company
ACC
Bombay Dyeing
Ballarpur Industries
Ceat Tyres
Century Spinning
Food Specialities (now Nestle)
Great Eastern Shipping
GSFC
Glaxo
Gwalior Rayon (now Grasim)
Hindustan Aluminium (now Hindalco)
Hindustan Lever
Indian Hotels
Indian Rayon
ITC
Kirloskar Cummins
Larsen & Toubro
Mahindra & Mahindra
Mukand

Pieco Electronics (now Philips)
Premier Automobile
Reliance Industries
Siemens
TELCO (now Tata Motors)
Tata Power
Tata Steel
Voltas
Zenith

(Source: PIB press release in 2010, https://pib.gov.in/newsite/erelcontent.aspx?relid=56659.)

Appendix 5

Foreign and Technical Collaborations Asian Paints Entered in the 1980s and 1990s

Table E1: Asian Paints foreign collaborations through the 1980s and 1990s

Year	Foreign Partner	Product/area
1985	Devoe Marine, USA	Marine and other protective coatings
1985 and 1992	Nippon Paints, Japan	Automotive, powder coating and coil coating
1986	Wacker Chemie, Germany	Phthalic anhydride
1992	Sigma Coating, Netherlands	Marine offshore and high performance
1993	PPG Industries, USA	Electro-deposition, coating products

(Source: Annual reports)

Table E2: Asian Paints benefits of technical collaborations

Product	Client/industry
Epoxy paints	Indira Gandhi Centre for Atomic Research Kaiga Nuclear Power Plant
Coil coatings, powder coatings	Coil coatings (Nippon Denso Ispat, Shree Precoated Steel), washing machines (Onida, Videocon)
Marine and offshore high-performance coatings	Engineers India Limited, Larsen & Toubro
Pre-treatment chemicals, paints, plastics, etc.	Automobile sector (DCM Daewoo, Maruti Udyog, Bajaj Auto, Kinetic Honda, Hero Honda)

(Source: Annual reports)

Appendix 6

Sensex Exits (1991 to 2001)

Table F1: Stocks belonging to family businesses that exited from the BSE Sensex over December 1991 to December 2001

#	Company	Group	Comment
1	Aditya Birla Nuvo	Aditya Birla Group	Formed in 2005[1] by the merger of Indo Gulf, Birla Global Finance and Indian Rayon; the company was restructured again in 2017[2]
2	Ballarpur Industries	Thapar Group	Entered liquidation in 2022[3]
3	Bombay Dyeing	Wadia Group	-

[1] 'Aditya Birla Group | Media | Press Reports | A Landmark Restructuring', https://www.adityabirla.com/media/press-reports/landmark-restructuring, accessed on 6 January 2024.

[2] 'Amalgamation of Aditya Birla Nuvo with Grasim and Demerger & Listing of the Financial Services Business Approved by Shareholders Highlights', https://www.adityabirla.com/media/media-releases/amalgamation-of-aditya-birla-nuvo-with-grasim, accessed on 6 January 2024.

[3] http://bilt.com/liquidation/ accessed on 6 January 2024.

4	CEAT	Harsh Vardhan Goenka Group	-
5	Century Textiles	Aditya Birla Group	-
6	Futura Polyesters (earlier known as Indian Organic Chemicals)	BM Ghia and DS Dalal	Stock trading has been suspended by BSE[4]
7	GE Shipping	Sheth Group	-
8	Hindustan Motors	C.K. Birla Group	C.K. Birla resigned in 2013[5]
9	Indian Hotels	Tata Group	-
10	Mukand Limited	Bajaj Group	-
11	Premier Automobiles	Walchand Hirachand Group	Applied for bankruptcy in 2018[6]
12	Tata Power	Tata Group	-
13	Voltas	Tata Group	-

[4] https://www.bseindia.com/stock-share-price/futura-polyesters-ltd/futurapoly/500720/, accessed on 6 January 2024.

[5] Probal Basak and Ishita Ayan Dutt, 'What Next for CK Birla after Hindustan Motors?', *Business Standard*, www.business-standard.com, 11 June 2014, https://www.business-standard.com/article/companies/what-next-for-ck-birla-after-hindustan-motors-114061101349_1.html.

[6] Maulik Vyas, 'Fiat Padmini Long Gone, Premier Ltd Now Faces Bankruptcy', *Mint*, 13 December 2018, https://www.livemint.com/Auto/09yvO5wYAbWCBhbXvU9cnN/Fiat-Padmini-long-gone-Premier-Ltd-now-faces-bankruptcy.html.

14	Zenith Steel Pipes & Industries (earlier known as Zenith Birla)	Yash Birla Group	Net worth fully eroded as per 2022 annual report

(Source: List of stocks is from Exhibit 27, page 19 of Ambit Capital 2015 report titled 'Sensex exits', remaining data is from company and news websites, and annual reports)

Appendix 7

Notes on India's Family Business Construct

More than half[1] of new companies formed in India perish or become dormant. The 45 per cent that survive stay in business for more than twenty years. The statistics were probably tougher when Suryakantbhai decided to start his paints trading agency in the 1930s and reached out to his friends. Many entrepreneurs in India, thus, start a business but not all survive to see them succeed. The rewards for those who succeed—like Suryakantbhai and Champakbhai did—can be huge. Family businesses[2] (or FBs) make up more than 90 per cent of the world's enterprises and some of the largest brands in the world (from LVMH to Rupert Murdoch's News Corp) are FBs.

But what is an FB? Anyone who has seen the hit HBO series, *Succession* would have an idea and probably more than half an interest just for the drama. Beyond the simple definition of a business owned by a family, there are usually three pre-requisites—the presence of at least one family, usually linked by

---

[1] Sourabh Gupta, 'India Inc's Survival Rate', *Economic Times*, https://economictimes.indiatimes.com/markets/stocks/news/india-incs-survival-rate/survival-of-companies/slideshow/71076821.cms.

[2] Staff, 'The Resistible Lure of the Family Business', *The Economist*, 6 April 2023, https://www.economist.com/business/2023/04/05/the-resistible-lure-of-the-family-business.

blood, a family and business that has thrived beyond the first generation and majority ownership of the company.

The Myth of the Third-Generation Curse

The third generation—which would play an important role in the Asian Paints split—is apparently jinxed, at least in popular culture. 'Shirtsleeves to shirtsleeves in three generations' is a familiar saying in American business history, often attributed to the famous industrialist Andrew Carnegie[3] but not found in his writings. Similar variations are found in other cultures as well, such as Scotland which has, 'the father buys, the son builds, the grandchild sells and his son begs', China with 'wealth never survives three generations' and Japan with 'rice paddies to rice paddies in three generations'. There is, in all probability, an Indian version as well. Many websites attribute the original saying to a proverb from Lancashire, 'clogs to clogs in three generations'.

Does the third-generation curse[4] apply to India? Not really. Let's take a look at history. The British Raj and the licence raj valued connections and the possession of a licence over merit, talents, managerial skills, etc. Hence, reputation and pedigree mattered more than anything else and was a barrier to entry. Even expansion had its limits, and once the founder passed away, dividing his various businesses would lead to disputes.

Large groups that flourished during the British Raj floundered after Independence. Professor Roy writes,[5] 'Between 1952 and 2000, almost all the major business groups split, usually among brothers and not always in a friendly fashion. In the colonial era, few cases of succession disputes and splits can be found.'

---

[3] https://www.oxfordreference.com/display/10.1093/oi/authority.20110803100502580

[4] Satish John, 'The Third-Generation Curse: Myth or Reality?', *Mint*, 31 January 2010, https://www.livemint.com/Politics/CQpCCFxCEfmhu4H1WtakvK/The-thirdgeneration-curse-myth-or-reality.html

[5] Tirthankar Roy: *A Business History of India*.

Closer to Champakbhai's era, Professor Tripathi estimated[6] that there were around thirty splits between 1979 and 1989, most of which were marked by acrimony and rancour. The fact that these splits happened when Champakbhai was in his sixties meant there is a good chance that they played on his mind.

Here are a few high-profile splits that could have left an impact on him:

a) Following G.D. Birla's death in 1983, there was[7] a family settlement of the various businesses,
b) The Walchand Hirachand group split[8] in 1992 after many years of staying together,
c) The Mafatlal group, at one time the third largest after the Tatas and the Birlas, split in 1979,
d) The three sons of Kamlapat Singhania split in 1979, and
e) The Shri Ram Group split between Lala Shri Ram's three sons in 1984.

Risk of Obsolescence

Infighting and disputes are one way for FBs to decline. Another risk is the failure to adapt to changing times, with external factors such as economic reforms and technology. One way to gauge how families respond to such externalities is to track their presence in the benchmark stock market indices like the S&P BSE Sensex 30 (or Sensex) and the NSE Nifty 50 (or Nifty).

---

[6] Ranju Sarkar, 'The Changing Face of Family Business Splits', Rediff, 8 September 2010, https://www.rediff.com/money/report/the-changing-face-of-family-business-splits/20100908.htm.

[7] T.N. Ninan, 'After Months of Tension, Birlas Part Ways Amicably', *India Today*, 20 December 2013, https://www.indiatoday.in/magazine/economy/story/19870930-after-months-of-tension-birlas-part-ways-amicably-799365-1987-09-29.

[8] Anusha Subramanian, Dhiman Chattopadhyay and Suman Layak, 'The Empire Crawls Back', *Business Today*, 15 March 2010, https://www.businesstoday.in/magazine/special/story/the-empire-crawls-back-17525-2010-02-15.

These indices track the size of a company based on market capitalization which, in turn, depends on factors like financial performance. The Tatas and Birlas, for example, have been around for more than 100 years and still find many of their companies (e.g. Tata Steel, Grasim) in the benchmark indices.

Now, we know that the 1991 economic reforms benefited India but also left many legacy businesses in tatters because they could not respond to competition. Let's assume Champakbhai could foresee which FBs would leave the Sensex between 1991 and 2001—the decade post economic reforms. What would he see? He would see that an astonishingly high eighteen of thirty companies in the Sensex had left the index by 2001 (Appendix 6). Some of these belonged to people he knew and respected.

A few of them faded away, such as Ballarpur Industries, Futura Polyesters, Hindustan Motors, Premier Automobiles and Zenith Steel Pipes. All of these belonged to large business families; the founder of Futura Polyesters (earlier known as Indian Organic Chemicals) B.M. Ghia was on the Asian Paints board for a long time in the late 1970s and 1980s.

Some of the companies mentioned above have had to rely on their land (usually a prestigious asset sold only in emergencies) to survive and transform from their original businesses that were swept away by the winds of change. Cotton mills in Mumbai, for example, had to be relocated.

Family disputes do not play out well in the public eye, especially when reputation and prestige are of utmost importance to families. All the benefits and advantages of FBs can be destroyed by ego, pride, ignorance and arrogance. It was thus only natural for Champakbhai to keep this in mind when he was in his late seventies in the years leading to the split in 1997.

Acknowledgements

This book was possible with the support of Champakbhai's son, Atul Choksey. Atul introduced me to the Choksey family, namely a) his elder brother Girish Choksey and his wife Sunita Choksey, as well as their sons Ankur and Prashant; b) his elder sister Rita Parekh; and c) his younger brother Amit Choksey and his wife Priti Choksey. I am grateful to all of them for giving me so much of their time and being candid with many stories about Champakbhai. Thanks for the many meetings at home and their respective offices. The Chokseys, in true Gujarati spirit, were extremely warm hosts, and I was honoured to meet them and partake of their hospitality at their home, Geetanjali.

Atulbhai and his wife, Parul Choksey, spent time over many meetings talking about Champakbhai's early life at home and his initial days with 'Asian' (as Asian Paints was referred to in almost all my meetings for this book) in its early years. As is the case with many successful entrepreneurs, their work becomes their life and—as the Upanishads put it—takes them from deepest desire to destiny. For Champakbhai, Asian was his life, as was evident in conversations with his family.

My gratitude to Atulbhai and Parulben for their generosity of time and willingness to share CHC's story and many of the photographs in this book, especially the brilliant painting made by R.K. Laxman for CHC, with Gattu standing by. That colourful painting is indeed a great tribute to a great entrepreneur drawn by India's greatest cartoonist.

Atulbhai introduced me to many friends and well-wishers of Champakbhai such as Devendra Kothari who was managing director at Kansai Nerolac and a veteran of the paints industry. Devubhai was kind enough to write a personal tribute for Champakbhai in this book, and I am thankful to him for his time. Similarly, thanks to K.M. 'Kanubhai' Sheth, chairman of Great Eastern Shipping, for his recollections of walking with Champakbhai at Worli Sea Face and recounting many other stories; and thanks to Jayant Gandhi, the owner of the plot of land at Matunga which would house Asian Paints' first large facility before it shifted to Bhandup.

Asian Paints was born in Bombay (as Mumbai was called then) and the history of that era was brought alive to me by that quintessential Mumbaikar, Bharat Gothoskar of Khaki Travels. Bharat introduced me to senior heritage activist and researcher, Jagdish Gandhi, who spoke to me about the history of areas like Girgaum, Kalbadevi and Pydhonie where Champakbhai stayed and where Asian Paints had its initial facilities. Thanks also to another quintessential Mumbaikar, Naresh Fernandes, for sharing his knowledge and perspective on Bombay in the pre-independence era.

Before I began work on this book, I spoke with Sundeep Khanna of *Mint* and Harish Damodaran of *Indian Express*. Sundeep's biography of Azim Premji (*Azim Premji: The Man Beyond the Billions*) was shortlisted for the Gaja Capital Business Book Prize in 2021, and Harish's book on Hatsun Agro (*Broke to Breakthrough: The Rise of India's Largest Private Dairy Company*) won the same award in 2022.

I thank them for their valuable and very useful guidance for my book. Anyone who writes a book on India's businesses and its entrepreneurs—especially the older generations—has my gratitude. There isn't much out there on these topics and these stories (especially the older stories) are probably written as a labour of love. To write a book in an age of short attention spans speaks of a high level of passion.

A massive thank you to Chinmay Tumbe, associate professor of economics, Indian Institute of Management Ahmedabad.

I have rarely met anyone as passionate as him about India's corporate history. It was an honour for me to walk the beautiful campus of IIMA. Thank you, Chinmay, for the tour. As a young graduate in the 1990s, I could not clear the CAT, so you'd understand why this was a big moment for me. Much of the research of this book is based on the old annual reports of Asian Paints which I was lucky to get access to at the Vikram Sarabhai Library at IIMA. A big thank you to the librarian and the staff for their invaluable help.

And now, the core group of ex-employees at Asian Paints on whose memories, recollections and anecdotes this book rests. This is a veteran group of people who spent decades at the company back in the 1960s, 1970s, 1980s and 1990s—the era when Asian Paints built its moats that kept it number one, increasing the distance with competition every decade.

I'll start with Biji Kurien. Biji introduced me to many ex-employees of Asian Paints, most of whom have been quoted in this book. I met Biji for the first time back in 2015 when I was working with Saurabh on *The Unusual Billionaires*. When I met him eight years later, it seemed like 2015. Behind Biji's warm smile and gentle laughter is his razor-sharp memory that recollected many stories with verve and clarity.

I've generously borrowed from Biji's interviews and his book, *Half a Century and Still at the Crease*. Biji is a paints industry veteran and an active IIMA alumnus and it was my honour to spend time with him. I am thankful to Biji for giving me so much of his time and patience and also for treating me to great coffee and breakfast in Chennai.

I am also thankful to T.N. Ramaswamy, Biji's batchmate from IIMA for his recollections of Asian Paints and Champakbhai that form part of this book.

I met P. Mohan Murty in Hyderabad over a long breakfast. He was the first managing director and chief executive officer at Asian Paints who was not from the founding families. He was followed by K.B.S. Anand and Amit Syngle. P. Mohan

Murty joined Asian Paints in 1971 and retired in 2012, and his recollections of his time at the company as well as his many interactions with Champakbhai at work are extremely important for this book, for which I am grateful.

I am very thankful to Pramesh Khanna who joined Asian Paints in 1962 and worked there for forty-two years. He spoke with me over the phone since he's based in New Zealand. I am grateful to him for sharing the note he prepared for Asian Paints when he retired. Asian Paints scored many early victories overseas—another first for an Indian paints company—and I am thankful to Pramesh Khanna for sharing his memories with me.

Similarly, I am thankful to both V.S. Ram and Jagdish Acharya—both of whom spent many decades at Asian Paints, interacted with Champakbhai and are associated with the Paints and Skilling Council. I met them in Mumbai and over the course of our meetings, I learnt a lot about how Asian Paints expanded its manufacturing operations in India as well as overseas.

I met K.B.S. Anand in Mumbai and am thankful for the time he gave me and the many recollections and memories he shared. K.B.S. Anand took over from P. Mohan Murty as managing director and CEO in 2012. He is another career Asian Paints veteran who rose through the ranks and his recollections—especially the 'scariest incident in my life' anecdote—are important in bringing about the unique work culture that Asian Paints had built.

Another product and another leader of that work culture is Bharat Puri, managing director at Pidilite Industries. He is one of India Inc.'s most distinguished leaders and I am thankful to him for sharing his time and his detailed memory with me. He posited that Asian Paints is a CEO factory like HUL and rattled off a list of names that now form a table in Chapter Six of this book. I am indeed very thankful to Bharat Puri for spending time with me and sharing the many victories that he was instrumental in scoring at Asian Paints.

My trip to Bengaluru stands out as an important event for this book. On that trip, I was lucky to meet Veeraraghavan, the man behind Asian Paints' mainframe and his wife Lakshmi at their home. He walked me through the 1970s when the computer arrived in Bhandup and the long road in making computers and technology an integral part of Asian Paints operations. He also introduced me to Fausto Cardoso and M.M. Khan with whom I had an unforgettable lunch where all of them relived the good old days. I am thankful to them for sharing their many memories with me. I am also thankful to Sanjeev Aga for sharing his insights on his days at Asian Paints.

I am thankful to Asha Bhumkar and her daughter-in-law, Priya Bhumkar for sharing their memories of C.J. Bhumkar as well as the Choksey Family. Not much has been written on Asian Paints' technological prowess and Mr. Bhumkar played an important role in strengthening this area. Similarly, I am thankful to Pramila Kudva for sharing her recollections and memories of K.G. Kudva, another important part of the paints technology team at Asian Paints. My thanks also to Vivek Patwardhan for talking with me and for sharing his blog post on Chari.

Now, over to the industry experts, some of whom I am lucky to count as friends, who helped me understand many aspects. My thanks to Amrit Rekhi, head of industrial sales at Kansai Nerolac, who helped me understand how institutional sales work in the paints industry. Amrit also helped me get a better idea of the paints industry with important data and inputs.

My thanks to my fellow podcaster at IVM Podcasts, Ashdin Doctor, who introduced me to his father Vispy Doctor. Vispy is the founder of consumer understanding company, ORMAX, and he played an important role in the 'Mera wala cream' campaign. Over a cup of coffee at the Starbucks outlet at Carter Road, Bandra, Vispy shared insights from the research and studies done for that campaign and how Asian Paints understood the 'C' in FMCG.

Another fellow podcaster from IVM and my partner in *The Last Brand Standing* (TLBS) podcast is Ambi Parameswaran. Ambi is an advertising veteran and a prolific author. He is also an extremely insightful person with a great sense of humour. Just sharing the space with him on TLBS was an honour for me. Before I even started writing the manuscript for this book, I knew I'd need Ambi's help, so thank you Ambi for sharing your many insights and for being such a cool friend. Of course, thank you Amit Doshi of IVM Podcasts for introducing the two of us and greenlighting TLBS.

Thanks to Manish Kumar at Penguin Random House India for commissioning this book. I worked with Manish for *The Victory Project: Six Steps to Peak Potential* (co-authored by Saurabh Mukherjea, 2020) and for my first solo book, *The Wisest Owl: Be Your Own Financial Planner* (2022). Manish's energy, enthusiasm and efforts remain a driving force for this book. Thanks to the extensive and meticulous copy-editing by Yash Daiv which strengthened the heft of this book. Thanks to Neeraj Nath for thinking the cover of this book.

I have left the final space in this acknowledgements section for Saurabh Mukherjea. Thanks very much, Saurabh for giving me this rare opportunity. I am thrilled and honoured to write this book on an extremely important figure of corporate India. Thanks for your time and your endless help, ideas and constant support. Your continued belief in my abilities as an author remains a source of motivation for me. Thanks to you and the team at Marcellus, especially Rakshit Ranjan, with whom I had spent much time researching Asian Paints back in 2015. It was great to have Rakshit's support yet again for this book.

Scan QR code to access the
Penguin Random House India website